I0187744

THE FAILED JOKE OF THE VEILED PROPHET

How a Fake Illinois Klansman Became the Grim Symbol of St. Louis's Happiest Civic Celebration

GEORGE GARRIGUES

City Desk Publishing

Library of Congress Control Number: 2021908898

City Desk Publishing

480 Morro Avenue, Suite E
Morro Bay, California 93442

www.CityDeskPublishing.com

Production services by Booknook.biz
Printed in the United States of America

Table of Contents

THIS WAY TO THE BIG PARADE

1 No Fair, St. Louis

THE IMAGE TIPPED OVER on the cover of this book doesn't look as threatening as the untipped version (which you will see standing upright in Chapter 12). In the latter, the blank eyes stare straight ahead. THE IMAGE grips a pistol, holds a shotgun and is just itching to slam anybody with that truncheon in his belt. He is surely a nightmare vision of a racist killer.

But THE IMAGE, as he was presented in the *Missouri Republican* newspaper on October 6, 1878, was intended to be a joke. I don't know any other spoof in American journalism that has gone so sour. It's time to set the record straight, to go back to a different era, to St. Louis, Missouri, almost a hundred and fifty years ago.

Even earlier. To Great Britain in 1817, Berlin in 1821, to the battlefields of the American Civil War in 1860-1865, to the night riders of the Ku-Klux Klan in 1875.

And to the year 2000 — because it was then that THE IMAGE emerged in our time on Page 6 of a 204-page hardbound book called *The St. Louis Veiled Prophet Celebration: Power on Parade 1877-1995,* presented by the University of Missouri Press, which identified the specter as:

> 1. *The Veiled Prophet.* Woodcut from the *Missouri Republican,* October 6, 1878. Missouri Historical Society, St. Louis.

On the opposite page of the book was quoted the *Republican's* caption:

> The above steel engraving represents the original Veiled Prophet himself. *[Not a woodcut now?]* The artist has caught very cleverly the expression of benignant firmness on his countenance, and shown with rare fidelity the dignity of his attitude. . . . It will be readily observed from the accoutrements of the Prophet that the procession is not likely to be stopped by street cars or anything else.

Wait! See the four dots? That's academic shorthand for "we're deleting something here." What was deleted? (Twenty-eight words. How mysterious. I'll tell you what they were in Chapter 12.)

Power on Parade claimed that the weapons were a sign that THE IMAGE

> would not be stopped "by street cars" — whose workers had recently participated in a general strike — "or anything else." Probably written by a founding member of the Veiled Prophet organization, the description underlined the image's message that the Veiled Prophet parade was intended as an expression of class and racial control.

Such flapdoodle! That's a word from the era, meaning *nonsense.* There is no evidence I've seen that St. Louis streetcar workers participated in that 1877 nationwide stoppage on interstate railways. It was railroad men who went on strike, not city drivers whose passenger cars were pulled along by mules or horses. "We are perfectly satisfied," one streetcar worker told a *Globe-Democrat* reporter, adding: "We would like a little more pay of course and a little less work" *(Globe,* July 27, 1877). That work included collecting fares or driving teams from twelve to sixteen hours a day, including Sundays.

As for THE IMAGE's "message" or intent? You can make up your own mind about *that* as you read this book.

The Atlantic magazine nonchalantly copied THE IMAGE to its September 2, 2014, issue, claiming it was "meant to serve as a sort of empty shell that contained the accumulated privilege and power of the status quo." What's more, he "was armed with a shotgun and pistol and is strikingly similar in appearance" to a Ku Klux Klansman. [Emphasis by *The Atlantic.]*

(But wait, *The Atlantic!* The weapons were not loaded, and this fellow was simply acting a part when his picture was taken. I'll share the details in Chapter 8.)

In 2020, there appeared a 518-page! jeremiad called *The Broken Heart of America: St. Louis and the Violent History of the United States.* In it a Harvard University professor tells you on Page 159 that

> Clad in a white hood and robes, the "Veiled Prophet" first patrolled the streets of St. Louis on the night of October 5, 1878, a revolver in one hand, a rifle in the other, a bowie knife looped through his belt.

More flapdoodle.

Flapdoodle on parade, if you will, since nothing like that occurred on Saturday, October 5, or any other time in 1878. Or ever.

It gets more doodly: In summer 2021, sitcom actress Ellie Kemper was crowd-shamed on the internet because somebody "discovered" that twenty-two years earlier she had reigned (at age 19) as the Queen of Love and Beauty during a fancy hoedown put on by rich toffs in St. Louis (the Veiled Prophet Ball), the first instance of which I'll lay out for you in Chapter 16, in all its richness, rowdiness, and resilience.

Vidiots with computers quickly found THE IMAGE online and cast it as a photobomb alongside Kemper in reproachful YouTube videos. A Confederate flag waved in one of them, which is pretty lame considering this innocent poseur was photographed in Illinois, never a part of the Confederacy.

Social media took note. The hashtag *#KKKQueen* popped up. Kemper found it wise to post an Instagram *mea culpa* which said that the Veiled Prophet bunch "had an unquestionably racist, sexist, and elitist past. I was not aware of this history at the time, but ignorance is no excuse."

So here's a whole book to cure any ignorance concerning the origin of this Veiled Prophet myth. It's all true, too, except for Chapter 10, which is totally made up but is more true than anything else written recently about the early years of the VP because it is based on research and common sense, not on preconception.

Well, all right, you stipulate, but (louder) *What's the joke? Nothing funny about the KKK!* I'll get to that in Chapter 12, where THE IMAGE glowers at at us like evil incarnate, but, shucks! he's no danger to anyone. Not even to the bug, the lion, or the lady with the hot chocolate, alongside him.

In the pages to come, you'll read newspaper articles (set in an old-timey typeface very close to fonts used in the 1870s), written by reporters who were just as smart and insecure as you and me, but who lived a century-and-a-half ago and had a different way of looking at everything around them. They also used now-refashioned words, like *car* (a wagon or a mule-drawn streetcar*), corsage* (the bosom of a lady's dress or gown), g*irdle* (a belt around her waist), and *toilet* (her hairdo, makeup, and clothing).

The 19th Century was a time when every crossroads village seemed to have its own newspaper; the big cities might have three or four or five, or even more, in various languages. From St. Louis I bring you the *Missouri Republican* (sometimes called the *St. Louis Republican),* shortened to the *Republican;* the *St. Louis Globe-Democrat* and the *St. Louis Post*, which I shorten to, duh, the *Globe* and the *Post.* I omit the very influential *Westliche Post* and *Anzeiger des Westens* because I can't read their grotesque German *Fraktur* characters.

Stories are best told by those who lived them, so you'll savor the flavor of a bygone time, when journalists writing with pen and ink liked to josh with their readers if they felt like it, normally on the editorial or feature page.

Through the lived experience of professional but often playful reporters, we will explore the origins of the Veiled Prophet Parade and Ball and investigate the mythology around them. Together we'll meet a Persian bride known as "Tulip Cheek," a Confederate versifier and his carpetbagger brother, various versions of the Prophet himself, and even a phantom (who was partial to hot Scotch whisky). And of course we'll find out how a Ku-Klux lookalike in a pointy hat became immortalized as The Image, to be posed alongside winsome Ellie Kemper in modern computer feeds.

The St. Louis Veiled Prophet Celebration began its long run in 1878 as a big parade and fancy dance. Each year the daughter of a prominent businessman or social leader would be chosen as a "queen." She was crowned by a mysterious being called the Veiled Prophet. (Her official title became *Queen of Love and Beauty* around 1894, at the height of America's Gilded Age, when young society women were expected to do that and look like that.)

That procession has been succeeded by *America's Birthday Parade*, now part of a community celebration renamed *Fair St. Louis*. This popular frisky fair, a July jollity on the Mississippi riverfront, attracts up to a million people a year. Most everybody thinks it pure enjoyment—all those bands and floats, refreshment booths and souvenirs. And don't forget the masterful fireworks.

It's the same frolicsome event which, *The Atlantic* warned in 2014, had a "dark and sordid history." Oh, my!

The parade is gone. Yet up to a hundred thousand visitors did throng St. Louis each year for more than a century to enjoy the "arrival" of the Veiled Prophet and his mob. Special railroad trains were added. Cots were hauled into hotel rooms, or families slept in doorways. This "empty shell" of a hooded man, as *The Atlantic* called him, was so significant in St. Louis history that for decades "VP" could mean only one thing: *Veiled Prophet*. The parade was reinvented annually with a different theme for each new, enthusiastic audience.

We begin the story across the seas with an Irish poet who brought his own version of the Veiled Prophet to the attention of the western literary world.

2 Tulip Cheek

IN 1817, IRISH AUTHOR Thomas Moore published *Lalla Rookh: An Oriental Romance,* one of the most admired poems of the 19th Century. In the epic, a young woman named Lalla Rookh ("Tulip Cheek" in Persian) is carried in a desert camel caravan across many leagues to wed a prince. During the journey, a handsome storyteller, Mokanna, spins four tales for her, including "The Veiled Prophet of Khorassan." Tulip Cheek falls in love with the storyteller, and then, surprise! he turns out to be the prince (in disguise) whom the woman was on her way to marry.

The masterwork, heavily researched and footnoted, was a world-wide hit — so much so that parts of it were translated into Persian, leading Moore's friend, Mr. (probably English poet Henry) Luttrell, to gibe in a quatrain:

> I'm told, dear Moore, your lays are sung,
> (Can it be true, you lucky man?)
> By moonlight in the Persian tongue,
> Along the streets of Ispahan?

The latter being a city in Persia (modern Iran).

The poem was a hit in Regency Britain. The London *Morning Post* said this:

> **(May 30, 1817.)** Few works within our recollection have excited such ardent anticipations of pleasure as the *Lalla Rookh* of Mr. Moore, and which, from the novelty of its plan, is calculated to become a subject of future interest and controversy with the public.
>
> The first, and most imposing, poem is the *Veiled Prophet of Khorassan,* founded on the mission of an impostor, who, in the year of the Hegira 163, pretended to support Mahomet. It opens with the description of this new usurper, Mokanna, who, enveloped in a mysterious veil, continues to make a triumphant progress, alluring to his standard crowds of deluded votaries. . . .
>
> Indeed, the whole is of a dramatic cast. . . . the scenes produce an almost theatrical impression on the imagination.

A *theatrical* impression! Just as today our best-sellers are made into popular motion pictures, in the 19th Century books and poems went onto the popular stage. In England and on the Continent, tastemakers wasted no time in interpreting, or misinterpreting, the mysterious Veiled Prophet.

The Royal Theatre (Astley's), near London's Westminster Bridge, publicized its 1820 version as a "Splendid Oriental Romance, with new Scenery, Machinery, Costume and Horse Evolutions." It was an "entirely new Equestrian Spectacle Melo-drama" that featured:

> Zelica, Mrs. Astley. — Surprising Horsemanship by the Young Austrian, without Saddle or Bridle. — Extraordinary Dancing and Equilibriums on the Tight Rope, by Monsieur Longuemare, from Paris. — Vaulting and Tumbling.

> — The whole to conclude with GIOVANNI IN THE COUNTRY; or, A GALLOP TO GRETNA GREEN.

A correspondent sent this from Berlin, Prussia:

> ***(Morning Chronicle*, London, February 27, 1821.)** We had a most splendid Court festival. It took place in the state rooms of the Castle Royal, where the (so called) white hall, and the adjoining apartments, had been fitted up for it. The idea of this exhibition of royal pomp is from Moore's beautiful poem, *Lalla Rookh.*

The imposing result: a series of *tableaux vivants,* or "living pictures." On a special stage, in front of four thousand spectators, costumed royals and nobles posed motionless in

> scenes from the four poetical narratives interwoven in the poem, viz. that of the Veiled Prophet of Khorassan, that of the Peri and the Paradise, that of the Ghebers, and last, that of the Feast of Roses.
>
> Each of these dramatic performances (if you may call them so) was preluded by a song, containing a narrative of the scenes which the spectators were to behold. These songs, from the pen of Dr. Spiker, the Royal Librarian, were admirably arranged by the Chevalier Spontini, the leader of the band royal, who had also composed the introductory march and the music for the ballet, with which the whole finished.... The entertainment was most splendid....

From the beginning, this "Veiled Prophet" sensation was adapted for public fun, with horses, dancers, costumes, royalty, and special effects — as it would later be in America. (We will, in fact, see a New Orleans *tableau vivant* in Chapter 4.)

Newspaper readers in the U.S.A. quickly learned about the Prophet.

> (*Mississippi Free Trader,* September 24, 1817.) An imposter named Mokanna arises in Persia under the pretext of destroying Mohammedanism and appears in a silver veil, which he puts on to conceal the divine radiance of his countenance, that no mortal can look at without perishing, but in fact to cover his ugly phiz, which the poet seems to wish his readers to believe that of a monkey, or something still more monstrous.
>
> (*Lancaster, Pennsylvania, Intelligencer,* December 6.) Lalla Rookh! Lalla Rookh! Nothing is talked of, among the Lovers of Poetry, but Lalla Rookh. It breathes the soul and fire of poetry; and the first part, the "Veiled Prophet," the only thing we have yet read, is worthy of Moore; it is written with great spirit. Had he done nothing besides the *Veiled Prophet,* this alone would give immortality to the name of Thomas Moore.
>
> ☞ The above interesting Work may be had at Dickson's Bookstore. Price, 1 dollar.

❦ ❦ ❦

Soon we will meet a very American counterfeit of Moore's Mokanna—a Louisiana Veiled Prophet—but first we need a bit of background, about the Slayback brothers.

3 Alonzo Slayback

ALONZO SLAYBACK WAS THE MAN who dreamed up the story line for the Veiled Prophet Parade, and it's a good bet that he wrote most of the publicity that ended up in the newspapers in 1878.

He was forty years old then, and he had had a truculent life.

Of the surviving children born to Anna Maria Minter Slayback, brothers Alonzo ("Lon," as he was called), was born in 1838; Charles E., in 1840, and Preston, in 1842. The last makes just two appearances in this book because he moved to Colorado.

Their father was Alexander Slayback, a Missouri lawyer. He died in 1848, age thirty-one, leaving her with the children.

Anna brought up the kids in Lafayette County, Missouri, about fifty winding miles on an unpaved road from Kansas City. She home-schooled all of them, but at age ten Alonzo was sent to the Masonic College in Philadelphia, Missouri. He graduated as a teenager with the equivalent of a bachelor's degree, with high honors.

This smart young man took off for St. Louis, on the eastern edge of the state at the Mississippi River, some two hundred miles from home. He became a lawyer.

Lon was a rebel from the outset, and a pugnacious sort, not admiring Northerners one little bit. At the outbreak of the Civil War in 1861, Missourians were divided: Some fought and suffered for the North and others for the South.

Alonzo for a time lived in St. Joseph County; he became

well known there. He made what one editor called "incendiary" speeches urging wary listeners to join the Confederacy; the thugs who accompanied him beat an onlooker "until he was apparently dead," accosted a man with "long, poetical locks," and cut off all his hair.

Slayback went off to join slaveowner and "General" J.O. Shelby's gang of ruffians. These bushwhackers killed and burnt out Yankee sympathizers in Kansas. The editor of the *Troy, Kansas, Chief* recalled on August 6, 1868, that Slayback also assisted in "ravaging Missouri."

In September 1861, Slayback was elected colonel of the 2nd Cavalry Regiment (later called "Slayback's Lancers"), under Sterling Price's 5th Division of the Missouri Guard, which fought for the Confederacy.

At the Battle of Fort Davidson, Missouri, (September 1864) Alonzo sent the defending Union commander a note that the black civilians within the fort would be massacred if captured. Whether this was a threat or a warning didn't matter: The federal cohort, including the civilians, snuck out after midnight, leaving twenty thousand pounds of gunpowder behind which they stacked in a pile and exploded via a slow-burning fuse.

Slayback fought 55 battles, but with defeat in 1865, Shelby and what remained of his unit galloped off to Mexico. As their horses splashed across the border, the crowd paused to ceremoniously drop their Confederate flag into the Rio Grande. Lon, who was a not-bad versifier, wrote a fulsome poem about it. "The glorious flag of the vanquished brave, No more to rise from its watery grave!"

In Mexico, Shelby tried to get his men hired as mercenaries. When that didn't work out, he sold the gang's artillery to a warlord for $16,000, divided the cash among his remaining troops, and let them all go.

Lon stayed behind a while, composing homesick verses in English (panegyrics to his wife and baby daughter, Susie) and trying to learn

Spanish, but eventually he took a ship to meet his mom. She had sailed to Cuba, where she talked him into returning to St. Louis.

Slayback was bitter about the South's defeat. He was a writer by inclination and talent. Among his many poetic compositions, he laid out the idea that the War Between the States was caused by Northerners and black people:

> 'Twas Northern men said, "Let the Union slide."
> They took good care to sell their negroes first,
> Before they found that slavery was a sin;
> They pocketed the cash with pious thirst —
> To soothe their consciences they squeezed *the tin.*
> I never heard of Yankee who durst
> Not keep the price the Southerners paid in
> For these same woolly-heads, who've been
> The real cause of all this war-like din.

He wrote a paean also "To Jefferson Davis in Prison," groaning that the conquered Confederate president, who had become the "prostrate defender of all that was holy," was being guarded in his cell by "a base menial slave" with an "impudent gaze." (The phrase "impudent negro," was current in the white man's jargon of the time.) Slayback's verse prophesied that Davis would "soon be a martyr, heroic, divine . . . And centuries hence . . . *[the world would]* honor the hero who now wears the chain."

In another postwar verse, dedicated "To Our Southern Belles," he complained:

> Tho now we've no coachman to send with our note
> (For the North has found need for his wisdom and vote),
> Yet the fellow who bears it I reckon will do,
> As he serves me quite well since he left off the blue.

This apparently means that his black servant has been freed from slavery and has gone off to Washington to become a Member of Congress. Further, his new coachman is an obsequious ex-Union soldier (maybe white, maybe black) who no longer wears his blue uniform.

Slayback composed an ode directed "To a 15th Amendment Politician." (This amendment to the Federal Constitution in 1870 attempted to give formerly enslaved men the right to vote.) He suggested that this elected rascal should:

> Go breathe the Afric scented air,
> Frequent polluted spots,
> Caress the rabble everywhere,
> Be friends with drunken sots. . . .
> Shrink from the gaze of decent man,
> Compound with vice and shame;
> Get office, steal, take gifts, and then
> Call this success and fame.

One of his poems claimed that Northerners stole from the South the custom of decorating military graves. All the Rebs loved him. Loved his poems, too. Unionists? Not a bit.

With the Confederacy dead (except in the minds of just about all Southerners), Alonzo Slayback was forgiven as part of Abraham Lincoln's exhortation about malice (toward none) and charity (for all). To get the latter, Slayback had to sign an oath to defend the United States Constitution.

He went back to politics, on behalf of the Southern Democrats. These were white Americans who couldn't stand Lincoln (a Republican), or Lincoln's policies, or anything to do with assuring civil rights for black Americans in the South, or anywhere else.

In 1868, Slayback was making speeches for Missourian Frank

Blair, who was the running mate of Democratic nominee Horatio Seymour in the Presidential election.

To put it bluntly they were all racists. (The Schomburg Center for Research in Black Culture in Harlem can show you a Seymour-Blair campaign badge with the motto *"This is a White Man's Country; Let White Men Rule."*)

Lon Slayback told listeners in a Buchanan County speech that he remained a rebel and that only by electing the Seymour-Blair ticket could "God's chosen people, the noblest men who ever lived, the gallant sons of the South" gain what they had fought for.

Seymour got 2.7 million votes across the nation to Ulysses S. Grant's 3 million, and he lost that year. But "God's chosen people" were going to win anyway in the South because in 1877 Reconstruction ended. Beatings, rapes, and murders of blacks intensified.

In 1876, smart-mouth Alonzo ran for the Democratic nomination in St. Louis's Second Congressional District to replace the incumbent, Erastus Wells, also a Democrat. Slayback succeeded in getting the endorsement of a number of political clubs but he was not yet the official candidate, though he thought he was. He was not polite about it. In a street-corner speech this happened:

> **(*Republican*, October 27, 1876.)** A large and exciting meeting was held last night at Seventeenth and O'Fallon streets, under the auspices of the Vinegar Hill Seventh Ward Democratic Club.
>
> Colonel A.W. Slayback was introduced as the first speaker and made an enthusiastic address. Mr. Wells, he said, had used his fifteen years in the City Council for the aggrandizement of himself and his d—d little street railroad *[the Missouri Railway Company, whose president he was]*. After going on at a rather lively rate for some time, he characterized Mr. Wells as a humbug and called him the

center of crooked and corrupt Democracy, if there was any such Democracy.

In those days, Democracy with a capital D referred to the politics and attributes of the Democratic Party.

Slayback thought things had come to a pretty pass when a lot of thieves and scoundrels could say, after a man had got the nomination *[that would be Slayback himself, he decided]*, that his name shouldn't be put upon the ticket. He characterized the action of the executive committee as an outrage. If Wells should be elected, the colonel announced his attention to follow him to Washington and unseat him if he had to walk there.

The speaker was sorry he had no time to go into national questions, but a little plain talk was necessary. Some people didn't like it when he, Slayback, called a spade a spade. They thought it was not polite; but the kind of treatment these fellows had been giving him did not entitle them to polite treatment.

The crowd shouted for the honorable Erastus Wells, who had been listening to this harangue. He came to the stand and said that after the "elegant language" that had fallen from the mouth of the preceding speaker, he felt some hesitancy how to address the meeting.

Colonel Slayback walked around and took a position in front of Mr. Wells, whom he interrupted several times, and each time noisy fellows who seemed to take their cue from him would make enough tumult to drown a brass band. *[This kind of incivility might seem familiar to American video viewers of certain 2016 and 2020 presidential election debates.]*

A club officer asked Slayback to let the meeting progress

> in peace, whereupon the latter engaged in a loud diatribe as to the impossibility of gagging him.
>
> Wells was allowed to conclude his remarks, but no sooner had he stepped from the stand than Slayback remounted it. General confusion: Cries of "Git down!" "Go ahead!" "That'll do!" "You're getting too fly!" *["too arrogant"]* etc., etc., were heard on all sides. Slayback tried to look gracious, but lost his temper at the uproar and yelled, "When those damned rowdies get done, I'll go ahead!"
>
> When the uproar settled for a minute, he said, "Let the dirty blackguards howl! They can't keep me from being heard. I will be heard!"

Whatever. Slayback lost the election. He went went back to lawyering, and two years later, he became the imaginative force behind St. Louis's Veiled Prophet Parade and Ball.

(You shouldn't be surprised to learn that the managing editor of the *St. Louis Post-Dispatch* was to shoot and kill hot-headed Lon Slayback on October 13, 1882, when the latter, armed with a pistol and bearing a grudge, stormed into the editor's office. But that's outside the realm of this book. Look it up in Wikipedia.)

Next, the second member of Team Slayback.

4 Charles Slayback

AROUND 1856, CHARLES SLAYBACK, at age sixteen, had followed Alonzo to St. Louis.

He looked for work, and I am sure Lon helped him. What else are brothers for? It took two months for this middle brother to land a job in a "commission house," which was a place with a bunch of roll-top desks and revolving chairs where people bought or sold just about anything and, one hopes, made a profit.

The teenage Charley was good at doing whatever it was that his bosses wanted him to do. Good enough to get a raise to thirty dollars a month at the end of his first year. He learned a lot about the business, and four years later he was a partner, at age twenty-two. He was a go-getter.

The war between the North and the South began on April 12, 1861, and Missourians were picking sides.

> **(*Morning Herald*, St. Joseph, Missouri, August 19, 1862.)** Alonzo W. Slayback's brother, Charles, has been skulking in town, and Sunday night our German patriots arrested him at his mother's house and took him to military prison, where he had his choice to enroll himself *[in the Army]*, leave the State, or go to jail. *[Missourians of German descent were almost all opposed to secession.]*

> He declares that he will not fight against his brother, who is in the bushwhacking gang. His case will be disposed of by the authorities.

Two years later, Charles and the youngest brother, Preston, got around to registering for the federal draft, but they never served; they paid others to take their places in the Union army. Perfectly legal in that era: As in most wars, poor folks fought on behalf of the rich.

Thus Charley had plenty of civilian time to make money. Along with partner E.O. Stanard, he was in the river trade all during the war, importing vegetables and such into St. Louis.

In 1867, two years after Robert E. Lee surrendered to Ulysses S. Grant (and Shelby dunked the Confederate flag in the river), the partnership broke up. Stanard kept at it in St. Louis, but Charles Slayback river-boated to New Orleans (occupied by the U.S. Army) to make money in the Reconstruction era.

He worked to aid the new city government. In 1870 he was secretary of an "Electoral Jury of Fifty," which had the job of helping the youthful governor, Henry Clay Warmoth, put together a non-Confederate New Orleans administration. If there was any financial U.S. government largesse included, it's my guess that Slayback and his newcomer crowd did not turn it down.

Charley stuck around in New Orleans for seven years, as an importer and, later, board member of a bank. At one point the municipal Board of Aldermen rejected his bid to bring in sacks of flour and sell them to the city because of his "exorbitant prices." *(Times-Picayune*, April 23, 1869.) That was the single item of skulduggery I found to blot his record.

He joined the Mystick Krewe of Comus, a top-secret society that got together to generate a big Mardi Gras parade every year. In 1868 the parade theme was *The Departure of Lalla Rookh From Delhi.* It was a big hit.

> ***(New Orleans Daily Picayune,* March 1, 1868.)** The procession of the Mystick Krewe lacked the sunshine and rosy dawn of a Persian day, the flowing waters and wide expanse of the River Jumma, covered with barges and banners, to make it real. The splendid cavalcade represented the fabled departure of the Delhi princess to the land of Bucharia.
>
> The rajahs and Mogul nobility were typified in the splendid cavaliers who lent elegance to the procession. Here were maces of gold and silver battle axes, and the gilt pineapples glittered from the tops of the palanquins. Embroidered trappings decorated the elephants, who bore on their backs small turrets in the shape of antique temples, within which lay the ladies of Lalla Rookh.
>
> The characters were exquisite. One could almost imagine, as the litter of the Princess passed by, that he could scent
>
> The perfume breathing round,
> Like a pervading spirit — the still sound
> Of falling waters, lulling as the song
> Of Indian bees at sunset, when they throng
> Around the fragrant nilica, and deep
> In its blue blossoms hum themselves to sleep.

The procession over, the focus shifted to the Varieties Theater to watch a living tableau, an unconscious echo of the one in Berlin four decades earlier.

> From the first moment the doors were thrown open, carriages arrived to discharge their freights of beautiful women, dressed in the most elegant and elaborate toilets *[long gloves, to the elbows; low-cut gown; hair piled on head]*. Passing

into the parquet, dress circle, and second tier, and even into the gallery, they bade adieu to their escorts and, clustering together in one grand bouquet, made up in loveliness such a sight as was never witnessed outside our city.

The subjects of the first three tableaux were taken from "The Veiled Prophet of Khorassan" and represented "His Court," "The Oath," and "The Bouquet." The scene in which the oath was administered was rendered with vivid and startling effect.

The closing picture was the marriage scene in which the beautiful Lalla Rookh, clad in robes of silk, glittering with pearls and jewels, is crowned Queen of Bucharia, and the rose-colored bridal veil is flung on her head, but not before she has kissed the little amulet of cornelian which her father at parting had hung around her neck.

And so ended the tableaux of the Mistick Krewe for 1868.

At age 34, Charles Slayback stood five-eleven, had a high forehead, small nose, sharp chin, long face, and brown hair, according to his passport application of June 1874.

He had made enough wartime money so he could spend some of it taking his family to Europe. (Before he left Louisiana, his banking buddies lauded him as "one who [had] acquired a place in the first rank, and has ever been noted for his strict sense of honor, sound judgment, liberal views and enterprising spirit.") *(New Orleans Bulletin,* November 20, 1874.)

The family returned to New York harbor the next October. Then they went to St. Louis, staying at the Southern Hotel (the fanciest place in town, at Fourth and Walnut streets) until they could find a mansion of their own.

5 Promoting the Prophet

ST. LOUIS WAS ACCUSTOMED to big parades, dating back to French days, before the Americans took over in 1803. After all, it was the French who invented the word *parade;* it means "pompous show."

Editor Henry Boernstein wrote in the German-language *Anzeiger des Westens* issue of September 24, 1851, that in those older days:

> the military parades took place on the Place d'Armes, and in the afternoon there was dance and song; in the better families they assembled on Sunday evening to play a party of *piquet* or *l'hombre;* in short, here reigned that cheerful, lively Sunday, which we find in France and in all French possessions.

(Yes, German-born Boernstein wrote in English as well as in his native tongue. He was a learned person.)

On Saturday, May 29, 1852, the *Anzeiger des Westens* had this ad:

GARDE A VOUS!

Les Gardes Lafayette se rassembleront lundi prochain á 5-1/2 heures du matin, en Grand Tenue sur la place ordinaire pour l'exercise et la parade. Par ordre Geo. Meisner, Sgt. Jr.

That meant the Lafayette Guards would assemble in Full Uniform at the usual place at 5:30 Monday morning to do some drills and a parade. Many immigrants could read French because they were from Alsace, straddling the European language dividing line.

A memorable spectacle was a parade the next year on Tuesday, May 10, 1853. The venerable St. Louis Grays marching unit headed the procession, followed by the National Guard, the Continentals and the German Yeagers. It began at 3 in the afternoon and didn't finish until 6 at night.

Everybody stared with amusement at a phenomenon who had been billed as "The Infant Drummer." Pfftt! Just a kid about six or seven years old dressed in full uniform. Riding in a buggy along with the Continentals, he was beating a drum almost as big as he was. Women and girls showered him with petals from balconies along the route.

Year after year there were parades, military drills, and even "sham battles." Large groups of men in ranks swarmed city streets. Sometimes these semi-military manifestations caused disputes with harried horsecar drivers trying to keep to a schedule as ranks of uniforms swarmed in front. Their bells would warn the marchers: Clang! Clang! Clang! Get off the tracks!

The festive opening of the Eads Bridge on July 4, 1874, was another excuse for a pompous show. A procession stretched fifteen miles and disbanded on the west bank of the Mississippi. It may to this day have been the most joyful celebration that St. Louis has ever had.

Three years later, another big parade. The opening of the annual St. Louis Industrial Exposition on Monday, September 10, 1877, was a big draw. Thousands flocked in from miles around on especially cheap train tickets. Each of thirteen divisions represented a trade or "mechanical industry," like lubricating oils, reapers and mowers, stoves, tinworks and queensware (a kind of fine pottery). Merchants and businesspeople sponsored and dressed up their own individual wagons. Even labor unions had floats.

That brings us to 1878. Fifty million Americans were doing their damnedest to pull themselves out of an economic depression. (The rich weren't quite so rich, but they were still rich.)

Businessmen, lawyers, bankers, traders, got together to help in bringing St. Louis out of the slump. They focused on promoting the opening week of the St. Louis Industrial Exposition. They wanted to bring a hundred thousand visitors to town.

By then, Alonzo and Charles Slayback (Lon and Charley to their friends) were settled into the city's power structure. They were among the perhaps ninety to ninety-five percent of St. Louisans who were white, and the fewer who were rich.

Charley told everyone about the Veiled Prophet parade he'd seen in New Orleans and how he might snag all those props and costumes for St. Louis to do something similar. Sure enough, he struck a deal, and everything was shipped upriver.

The Important People in town who were organizing this event got a warehouse on Twelfth Street to be their secret HQ, their man-cave. Nobody was allowed to enter except them. But of course they admitted the men and women to do all the dirty work or intricate, specialized tasks that the upper crust couldn't manage themselves, or didn't want to.

The mystery suffusing the project was the idea of Alonzo Slayback, the poet: He invented a scenario for a "visit of the Veiled Prophets." He sent press releases everywhere.

At the beginning, his VP storyline was scattered. Sometimes there was just one Prophet; sometimes there was a coven — a whole bunch of Veiled Prophets led by a Grand Mogul.

Soon, Missourians were drowning in publicity about the big event. The huge event. The biggest and best event ever to hit town. Each newspaper vied with the others in outlandish stories.

Most of them were probably written by Lon Slayback. He hustled up or commissioned a drawing that he sent out all over the place, with accompanying message.

'THE VEILED PROPHETS" GRAND PA-
GEANT IN ST. LOUIS.

(Globe, **July 6, 1878.)** The mystic order of "Veiled Prophets" has announced an intent to appear in public, but their puzzle is as dense as ever, for no one knows who they are. What are their aims? Why are they together? Nevertheless, that they possess vast resources of wealth and power and number among them many men of commanding influence will be a tangible fact upon the night of October 8.

This mysterious convocation, after solemn deliberation, has determined to depart from their heretofore rigorous rule of exclusion and to appear in a magnificent nighttime parade.

For appointments, originality, and beauty of design of their carriages, for unique, grotesque, and fantastic costumes, these fabled glories of fairy land and the mythological splendor of the ancients shall stand unrivaled by any display of the kind ever attempted in the world.

The procession will be several miles long, its dazzling beauties made visible by myriads of glittering lights. For visitors to this city, the opportunity of witnessing its grandeur will be sufficient recompense for the travel.

Buy tickets from the Grand Oracle or any of the High Priests.

The publicity onslaught continued:

(Post, **September 3.)** A reporter was talking to a fair young lady the other day.

"Who are the Veiled Prophets," said he.

"I don't know," said she.

"Are they of seraphic, demonic, or human kind?" said he.

"Of human kind," said she, "but whether prophets of good or evil, I know not. I imagine that they are a grave, sober set of people. Prophets are always that way, you know. I suppose they have long, white beards and wear long, white robes, like the learned men of Israel."

Every city of the Old World has its grand carnivals and seasons of frolic and fun. In the New World, New Orleans and Memphis have their annual Mardi Gras. But St. Louis has never had a genuine spectacular street display combined with a universal jollification of her inhabitants.

Who are the members of this "Mystic Krewe"? The answer is a profound secret. All this is very much mixed up. The city is full of Veiled Prophets, and you may jostle against them in the streets all day, and all night, but no man knoweth of their rising up nor sitting down.

The Secret of the Temple

These beings, though, now have a local habitation. You might have seen the low, rakish building erected at the corner of Twelfth and Market. Many have supposed it was a tobacco factory, an addition to the City Hall, or a military headquarters.

No. It is none of these. This is the Temple of the Veiled Prophets.

Here they congregate. No stranger knows what is on the inside. Passers-by say they have heard the hum of human voices, a wild, unearthly laugh, or a rasping sound of a carpenter's saw. But living man or woman has yet to see any person go into the building or out of it.

The Veiled Prophets do not propose to remain in such seclusion. On the night of October 8, they will take possession of the streets — to engage in a procession the like of which has never been seen nor conceived of in any city of the New World.

The city will be illuminated, the night will be almost turned to day, and there will pass a wondrous caravan miles and miles in length.

The most ravishing music will fill the air. Ten thousand flambeaux and torches will pass from hand to hand. Hundreds of harnessed horses will draw golden chariots where maidens will sit as fair as the roses with which they will be crowned.

Never to Be Forgotten

All St. Louis may look forward to 8th October as an occasion never to be forgotten. A hundred thousand strangers are expected to add to the immensity of the carnival. Old, young, male and female, they will all have one night of wild, unrestrained revelry, and the Veiled Prophets shall have the honor of it all.

Neptune, from the ocean, will be there, and Jupiter, from Olympus, and Satan himself will rise from the infernal regions to join the mighty procession. There will be temples and thrones and golden balls as large as *[hot-air]* balloons.

Savage bulls will be taken from the fields, made gentle as calves and held subject by garlands of flowers in the hands of vestal virgins. You will see Aphrodite, Hecuba, Europa, Clio, Diana, Thalia and Euterpe, and musical Pan will come from where he sits among the reeds of the river and play upon his hickory whistle.

Above all will tower the "Veiled Prophet" himself — the father of all, the ruler of all, the Alpha and the Omega. He will reign from a throne of dazzling glory, drawn by half a hundred fiery steeds. *[Mules, more than likely.]*

> A dozen common men can sit upon his knee, three find shelter in each of his ears, and he will take the roof of a house for an umbrella. Around him will gather a host of his children, the lesser Veiled Prophets, who will be clad in brilliant armor and guard their chief from all indignity and assault.
>
> After the Grand Caravan shall have wound its serpentine length through the streets, the prophets will repair to the Chamber of Commerce, and the great ball will commence. It will be the wildest and best-attended ever. The most gallant sons and sires of St. Louis will take the hands of the fairest ladies of the land in the gladsome dance.
>
> The Prophets will guard their identities, and when morning dawns, the mystery will remain: Who were they?

Five days later, in another newspaper, more bunkum:

> ***(Globe,* September 8.)** We have at last seen the official, and therefore the conclusive, evidence that we have in our midst a mysterious brotherhood known to the outside world as the Veiled Prophets.
>
> Their dictum or proclamation is just out, in which their grand something-or-other (the characters are in the ancient Oriental) announces that on the night of October 8 they will celebrate their great festival. Although famous in Persia and along the banks of the Tigris and the Euphrates, the festival will be observed for the first time in the New World — in St. Louis, to which the Prophets are at present confined.
>
> Much has been written about this body of men, but very little that is reliable: All attempts to lift the veil that conceals them have met with such signal failure, or such limited

information as to be useless in gratifying the cravings of public curiosity.

Within the guarded precincts of their Arcanum they have been teaching secrets of philosophy and chemistry, magnetism, and the occult art of magic that during the Middle Ages gave rise to the belief that they were in league with the Devil.

The great festival of October 8 is the most celebrated of Oriental antiquity. Many nations, in imitation of the splendor of the ancient prophets of Persia, borrowed from them.

We should give the Prophets a sincere welcome to our city. They come to enrich us with the results of subtle science, with wealth unbounded, and with a pageantry so gorgeous as to entrance all that may behold it; to make us all happier and better, to present to our little ones a picture more enchanting than the dream of the opium eater and to our maids and matrons a brief respite from cares either serious or trivial.

They come to gild our city with a carnival of beauty and melody, but they ask that the vulgar eye of curiosity cease to invade their privacy. We can never learn the names of our benefactors, and so the mystery of the Veiled Prophets will endure forever.

Next, the *Globe* gives us a story about a spectral Veiled Prophet kidnaping an editor from the newsroom, wafting him through a solid wall, and scaring the daylights out of him before asking for a favor.

6 Lights Turned Blue

***(Globe*, September 22, 1878.)** At the mystic hour of 11:45 o'clock last night, as *Globe-Democrat* editors and reporters were putting the finishing touches to the work of the day, the absolute quiet was broken by the Police Reporter, who exclaimed:

"What's the matter with the gas?"

All eyes swung to the jets above. The Society Editor (although normally a lion in a ballroom) caught at his beard and became ashen pale.

"The—lights—are—turning—blue!"

So they were.

The flames which had retained their brightness throughout the evening had lost their lustre. Their silvery whiteness had become a disagreeable ghastly blue.

The Society Editor must have contrasted the news room's supernatural luminescence with something he was more accustomed to: the gentle gleam of light falling from many-jetted candelabras upon the snowy shoulders of *ravissantes* blondes and *charmantes* brunettes. He leaped from his chair and exclaimed: "I'm a goin'a git!"

The lights burned bluer and sank lower. A voice sounded forth in sepulchral tones: "No—you—don't—young—man!"

The editor fell pallid into his seat but saved himself from a faint by a free use of his vinaigrette *[ornamental bottle of smelling salts]*.

The lights diminished to the size of the jet that is kept burning all night in well organized newspaper offices to light the cigars of any reporter still around. There was just enough illumination to show that — a *materialization* was in progress!

Ghastly Figure From Nothingness

The atoms of light and darkness coalesced and gradually took the semblance of a man. Not an ordinary man, with flesh and blood and cutaway coat and soft felt hat and baggy trousers, such as are nowadays worn, but a huge thing in armor cap-a-pie *[head-to-foot]* with monstrous and mailed feet about size 16.

As it grew, its helmet threatened to break through the ceiling and knock into "pi" *[jumbles]* the metal type in the composing room just above.

The Ghost's visor was up, but a pale gray veil floated from its scalp far down upon breast and shoulders, yet the dimness of illumination kept secret the face of the stranger.

Now that the materialization had materialized, men's cheeks grew pale. The sudden invasion of the modern by the medieval was unexpected, unnatural, and unpleasant. They heard:

"Which one of you gentlemen is heaviest on the descriptive style?"

For once there was no apparent anxiety to lay claim to any journalistic honor.

Neither the hero of a score of hangings, nor the describer of untold dog fights, nor the daisy of a dozen ballrooms, nor the Headline Man who modestly makes artful alliteration — none claimed any proficiency in the word-painting line.

The pause that ensued was painful, and what intensified it was the Thing turning calmly from face to face, scanning each as though he would select his victim with no haste.

Having made his survey, he reached forth, placed his mailed glove upon the shoulder of his choice, and, presto! the lights turned white again, but both the Spirit and the Headline Man were gone.

Mysterious Transportation

When the wordsmith came to his senses, after being whisked through a solid brick wall, he found himself three blocks away, on Pine Street and under control of the mysterious visitor.

"You seem cold." It was a natural, even voice.

"Why wouldn't I be?" With trepidation.

"We can soon cure that." A pleasant remark, and the Thing guided his companion through the doorway of a popular resort.

The barkeeper looked askance as his veiled visitor called genially: "Hot Scotch for two!" So appropriate, and familiar, was the order that the Headline Man peered carefully: To his surprise, it was one of his most intimate friends.

"You must excuse the brusqueness with which I carried you off, old fellow, but" — in a murmur — "it's a way we Veiled Prophets have of doing business!"

He explained:

He was an active member of the Mystick Krewe, and he'd been ordered by the Sublime Hime-uk-amuk of the Eastern Hemisphere to act as advertising agent of the

Veiled Prophets. With his supernatural power (which he could assume and discard at will), he had lifted the Headline Man through space and bore him westward.

Yielding to pity, he had resumed his mundane shape to allow his unbidden companion to recover from his fright and answer the specter's question.

Which was:

Had the Headline Man ever observed that huge building on Twelfth Street just back of the City Hall?

Yes, was the answer.

Was he aware that therein lay hidden the mysteries and incantations of the Veiled Prophets?

Yes.

Had the Headline Man the hardihood to accompany his friend into that building, look upon its contents, and describe them in an article for the *Globe-Democrat?*

Well . . . oh, why not?

The journalist wanted to finish the lemon peel at the bottom of the tumbler, but — the Veiled Prophet resumed his ghostly guise, snatched him up, and carried him away. He heard the bartender cry "Say, mister, you forgot to —"

He couldn't distinguish the rest of the words, whatever they were.

The Spirit then ghosted the Headline Man into the Inner Sanctum, that warehouse where busy men were assembling wagons and trappings of the procession.

A dazzling scene met his eye. Was it fairyland? What did these creatures mean? Roaring lions dragged cars of wondrous beauty of form and color; horses harnessed to beauteous chariots belched fire and smoke, gold and silver gleamed everywhere.

The journalist looked up to see the top of the pillar against which he had been leaning. He perceived a monstrous face some three feet wide and a mouth that could swallow a man with ease. This creature's leg had been the "pillar" all along!

It looked more like a huge wickerwork giant which the Druids filled with men and burned by way of devotion than a creation of our 19th Century!

"Is this the Grand Mogul?" the reporter breathed.

"This is the Sublime Hime-uk-amuk," his friend corrected. *[You will see what it looked like on a parade float at the end of the book.]*

A Grand, Triumphant March

The Spirit explained all:

- The sole object of the Prophets was to get up an entertainment to provide the people with a night's enjoyment and to bring visitors from the countryside.
- The Prophets were a closed corporation, and the secrecy of the Masonic fraternity was as nothing compared to the inviolable faith with which they preserved all the mysteries of their craft.
- The very best merchants were interested in success, and the amount to be expended would be thirty thousand dollars or more. The illumination will cost at least fifteen dollars per minute!
- Finally, the Veiled Prophet explained how the *Globe-Democrat* man was to write up the affair: Whet the public's appetite, but make only the faintest suggestion

> of the glorious treats which the Mystick Krewe was preparing.
>
> The reporter gave his word, and he has kept it — a fact which will be borne out by the grand, triumphant march to be the principal feature of the festival, between sunset and midnight on the 8th of October.

This was all nonsensical clowning. But everyone was working hard. By this time, the costumes and props from New Orleans were ten years old, so there was much refurbishing, sewing, and painting going on. I don't mean to say that the so-called "elites" of St. Louis did any of this themselves. "Money talks" was a catch phrase as apt in the 1870s as it is today. The anonymous seamstresses, carpenters, grooms, and wagonwrights simply did what they were told, in return for cash at the end of the week.

Thus a waggish *Globe* reporter did his part in contributing to the VP foofaraw. In the next chapter I will tell you more about a rival: the *Missouri Republican,* which you will first see in its most dispiriting time and then farther along getting a scoop on the *Globe.* A big one, really the key point of this entire book.

7 The Big Fire and the Spiffy New Building

IN 1870, A FIRE BURNED DOWN the building housing the *Republican.* Here's how the *Globe-Democrat* covered it:

> ***(Globe,* May 25, 1870.)** The alarm was first given in the composition room, fifth story, where about thirty-five compositors rushed out, screaming "Fire!" Three of them broke in the door of the bindery, second floor, but they were driven out by the flames, which had so filled the space it was impossible to think of saving anything.
>
> The occupants of the editorial room at the time (about a quarter past eight), were Mr. Thomas Garrett, the erudite literary editor, and James Edmonds, the night editor. They supposed that the noise was occasioned by a fire outside the building and remained at their desks.
>
> In about five minutes, the smoke began to pour in. Mr. Garrett put on his hat, locked his desk, put the key in his pocket, and walked out like one going to a funeral. Mr. Edmonds kicked off his shoes, pulled on his boots, took out of his desk an extensively annotated copy of Kant's *Transcendental Philosophy,* and ran down just in time to clear the edge of the flames in the second story.

Yes, newspaper writers of those days were perfectly capable of making fun of anybody they chose to, particularly (it seems) journalists who worked for the competition, or *opposition,* to use the proper shoptalk.

> Mr. William Hyde, the managing editor, who had a valuable private library in his room, rushed up to save some of the books. He was accompanied by a self-possessed compositor named Fisk, who began to assist him in throwing volumes out the windows. They had not thrown out more than a dozen before their retreat was cut off, and they plunged through the fire.
>
> Mr. Hyde escaped with a few trifling contusions. Mr. Fisk was asphyxiated, fell twice to the floor in the midst of the flames, but by extraordinary presence of mind crawled desperately forward and got outside without serious injuries.
>
> Within less than ten minutes, the entire building was a great sheet of flames.

Small wonder that when a fireproof replacement structure was opened some nineteen months later the architects had placed an enormous tank for water on its roof.

✿ ✿ ✿

If you had a friend to escort you to and through this magnificent new structure, this is what you'd see:

On the top of the five stories, a billboard proclaims *"The Missouri Republican, Established in 1808."* A smoke stack leads from the basement to the roof, and atop it you'd spot the newspaper's avatar — a raccoon figure cut in sheet iron, mounted on a pivot and veering in every direction with the change of wind. It had been the symbol of the *Republican* since 1840, in honor of its fealty that year to presidential candidate William Henry Harrison, known as the “Old Coon.”

Your friend would push open the sturdy swinging doors on the corner and you’d both go inside.

On the ground floor you would see a counting room, where money is taken in, receipts given, and business done. Back issues of the newspaper are protected in a fireproof vault. Just off from the cashier’s desk you might notice brothers George and John Knapp, the owners, busy in their offices.

On the second floor is the job-printing department, active with work for outside clients. Brochures, advertisements, fliers, show bills, books, are scattered about. That's where you might be headed if you want anything at all printed — a flier, a poster or a ream of stationery for your business. There's an elevator, but your friend leads you up the stairs.

The big windows of the editorial room on the third floor look onto Chestnut Street. Reporters, editors, artists, and office boys keep the place busy, almost twenty-four hours a day. On a table are piled stacks of weekly newspapers from across Missouri and Southern Illinois (on the opposite side of the river from St. Louis), and there are daily papers, too, from New Orleans, Chicago, New York, and Washington.

Spittoons sit on the floor near most doorways, for cigar stubs and tobacco juice. At night, gas jets provide enough illumination for everybody to see, more or less, what they are doing.

If you're there at the right time, you can feel the building shake as the two massive R. Hoe & Co. steam-powered printing presses in the basement go to work, churning out the day's news. A score of women hoist stacks of papers, paste on labels, and send them out the back door, where drays (delivery wagons) wait to take them to drop-off points throughout the city and, via the railroad station, to the State and the nation.

In the alley, the newsboys clamor for their share, gather them under their arms, then run into the streets, calling out "Ree-PUB-lee-kan! Ree-PUB-lee-kan! Getcher latest! Paper, mister?"

Next: How The Image was conceived, posed, photographed, drawn, chiseled, and printed.

8 The Klan and Its Deadly Visits

"GOOD MORNING, MR. DACUS." The 35-year-old Texan stood at a breakfast table in a DuQuoin, Illinois, hotel Wednesday morning, August 18, 1875. The other man looked up from his newspaper.

"Good morning. You have the advantage of me, sir."

"My name is Cy Oberly. We knew each other in the South during the War."

"Tennessee?"

"Yes."

Joseph A. Dacus, 37, and Cyrus S. Oberly had been in the Confederate Army.

"Join me."

They sat together and recalled the days of fortifications, signal rockets, booming guns, and forced marches. Dacus had been a grocer, cotton broker, farmer, school teacher, poet, political stump orator, book salesman, chief engineer of a flatboat, and superintendent of a saw mill. Now he was a writer in St. Louis for, among other places, the *Missouri Republican.*

Oberly had been nothing but a dedicated journalist — and an eager volunteer for Texas and the Confederacy.

"We concluded to travel together," Oberly wrote for the *Chicago Times* (printed also on August 29, 1875, in the *Cairo, Illinois, Bulletin,* where his brother, John H., was the editor). His byline was *OCELOT,* just one word at the end of his articles. His companion used his own name, *DACUS,* as the sign-off for his reports in the *Republican.* That was the custom of the time.

The two hired a carriage to take them to the Southern Illinois town of Benton, in Franklin County, where a passel of Ku-Klux had been arrested after they rode into the night to flog a local politician and shoot up another one.

Dacus and Oberly jounced eastward along a narrow, 20-mile road with corduroy ruts through a swamp made by the Little and Big Muddy rivers. Broad fields of buckwheat lined it, and tobacco plants spread their green, narcotic leaves. They got to Benton around noon.

Many of us today think of KKK victims in terms of those photographs we've seen of African-Americans hanged or burned to death, surrounded by crowds of somber or cheerful whites. But in Southern Illinois' Benton and Williamson counties in the 1870s, there were no or few blacks, so the Ku-Klux criminals we're examining in this book are taking out their grievances only on their white neighbors. Edgar F. Raines Jr. in his study published in the *Illinois Historical Journal* (spring 1985) wrote that "The decision to terrorize particular notables undoubtedly represented private animus." That is, the victims did stuff that the assailants or their women didn't care for, like living in sin or taking advantage of other people. Often, it was family against family, spanning more than one generation.

The organizer of this copycat offshoot, formed around 1867, was Aaron Neal of Franklin County, an old member of the Southern Ku-Klux. He'd been a Union cavalryman and later was a lawyer, working from a saloon in the hamlet of Sneakout, Williamson County. (Yes, there really was such a place.) *(Globe*, August 31, 1875.)

The *Chicago Evening Mail* on March 27, 1871, said about the Ku-Klux that

> there is not a schoolboy who does not know that . . . its white victims, since the close of the war, to say nothing of the blacks, are numbered by the thousands . . . there is virtually no protection to life or property of persons who come under the ban of the order. The local authorities do not pretend to correct the evil, or attempt to punish the crimes committed, because too frequently judge and jury are members of the Ku-Klux themselves. . . .

This is what the assailants did in that distressed but fertile part of Illinois even then called *Egypt* (the southernmost counties, maybe from a Biblical allusion, and maybe not): Accuse their victims of some transgression and, in a formal written communication, promise a "visit" or a "punishment." Sometimes they wanted cash and sometimes they wanted to administer a beating, a whipping, or a lynching. They warned their victims to get out of town, or die.

On the night of December 14, 1871, about forty men "under military discipline," descended on John Baker's farm, Raines wrote. They drove away his family and burned the house.

Shortly thereafter they did the same to other farmers, burning haystacks, taking men from their homes and whipping them. One Williamson County resident who had gained title to the properties of tax-delinquent farmers received a visit. Under threat of "guest-of-honor status at a lynching," as Raines put it, the man returned the lands. The confident Aaron Neal boasted that his marauders never had been caught, "and they never aimed to be."

In Franklin County, these vigilantes were organized to avenge what they considered public wrongs. One of their chilling acts was the 1872 murder of elderly farmer Isaac Vancil, who, some said, was hosting a woman of low repute. Or, others claimed, the old man intended to disinherit some of his relatives.

The pack of horsemen wore white masks, streaked with red about the eyes and mouth, and long, white hats coming to a point — their horses covered with white cloths and trailing red and black tassels. They seized Vancil, rode into neighboring Williamson County, and strung him to a tree.

In spring 1875. wealthy farmer Milton Coit was told to move a fence he had put up because it obstructed a road. He was also directed to get rid of a woman who was living on his farm. He did neither. Two days later he was killed by a rifle ball fired from a thicket along the road. Other outrages followed, always preceded by a warning.

In August 1875, John Hogan had Hiram Sommers arrested for selling liquor to Hogan's son. A judge ruled Sommers guilty and fined him a hundred dollars. A few days later, Hogan discovered a notice on his grounds demanding he hand over a hundred bucks to Sommers for the fine and more for the defense costs.

Hogan was captain of the Franklin County militia, so he was the wrong fellow to be threatened. He procured arms from Governor John L. Beveridge and formed a posse.

Around that time, modest, sooty blacksmith William Jacobs of Crawford's Prairie was visited at his forge by "the white-robed Ku-Klux, mounted and drawn up in line before his shop," the *Cairo Bulletin* reported in an unbylined article. The gang's leader, weapon drawn and flanked by his followers, demanded in a deep sonorous voice that Jacobs "Dance!"

> **(August 29, 1875.)** The frightened Jacobs, with perspiration rolling down his cheeks, commenced a grotesque shuffle in his leather apron from shoulders to knees. "Stop!" he heard. "You are a better blacksmith than a dancer." But a

> recollection of Jacobs' childhood frolics evidently came upon the victim, for he folded his arms and glided into a waltz, muttering, "Now, boys, this ain't right, nohow!" Then he cavorted into a highland fling, all the while making an odd plea, babbling without stop.
>
> He begged the riders to let him join the band. He made himself understood: Some men owed him a debt, but they wouldn't pay. His visitors muttered among themseles, approved his plea, and in the glare of Jacobs' furnace, swore him in, shared the passwords, and gave him the garb of the order.
>
> All that was very funny to the robed and laughing Ku-Klux, but in the end it proved a dear dance to them because Jacobs proved a traitor to the gang.

Next, the same pack planned "visits" to the homes of other white families. First was to be farmer James Brown in Williamson County. He had been measuring the hoofprints of the nightriders' horses in an attempt to identify the marauders.

The Ku-Klux rode to Brown's house the evening of Monday, August 16, 1875, and, as Dacus recounted it in the *Republican's* issue of Sunday, August 22 (portions reprinted on August 23):

> The "night angels" came with peaked caps, white robes, ghastly masks, and other infernal paraphernalia. Against him some of the Klan held malice, and they had warned and threatened until he had fallen sick from sheer agitation, and his wife was tending him.
>
> They declared they had come to whip him. The wife pleaded and entreated them for all sacred and solemn considerations and holy ties to allow her to receive the chastisement, but for the love of the Savior to touch him not.

> Mr. Brown grew wild, reason fled, the fever came, and he raved so that they reluctantly rode away. All night long the poor man cried out "Ku-Klux! Ku-Klux!" and when the grey dawn streaked the East with the earliest gleam of light, the voice failed, the eyes became glassy and fixed in a lifeless stare . . . . he was dead!

By then the mob had already made their next social call.

At 2 a.m. on Tuesday, August 17, Sheriff James F. Mason and posse lay hidden outside the rural home of County Commissioner Jack Maddox, another who had been threatened and the wealthiest farmer in Crawford's Prairie, Frankfort Township. Fifteen men in long, white robes and high, white pointed hats rode up as silently as they could, in a column of twos — shotguns and pistols at the ready. They wore white masks.

"Halt!" Mason cried. The answer was a pistol shot from the leader of the mob, and then a volley from the rest. The intruders turned their horses. The sheriff fired his pistol and his men their double-barreled shotguns. All the interlopers escaped except one man, John Duckworth, bleeding from the neck, the side, and an arm.

"Oh, for God's sake," he cried, "pray for me, for I will die! Forgive me. If I live, I will never do it again!" (*Deseret News* of Utah, September 4, 1875.)

When the sun rose, masks—six of them bloody and riddled with bullets—littered the earth for a mile among the hoofprints.

> ***(Republican,* August 20, 1875.)** Thirteen uniforms are now in the possession of the sheriff. They are unearthly looking attires and well calculated to create alarm in the soul of anyone. . . .

The culprits were caught and locked up. Many were injured; they were allowed to recuperate in guarded hotel rooms, with Newton Welch of the local militia nursing them. An indignation meeting was called, resolutions denounced the outrage, and weapons were handed out from the governor's stockpile.

> ***(Chicago Tribune*, August 19.)** The scouts were divided into squads, and warrants were placed in their hands to search all suspected places for uniforms and disguises and to arrest the parties implicated. It is the determination of the best citizens of the county to suppress all further manifestations of Ku-Kluxism in their midst.
>
> Sheriff Mason said that he would lead if the good men would follow, but he would not go with a lot of scalawags who would run off and leave him in the lurch when the tug of war came.

Reporters Dacus and Oberly got to Benton, the county seat of about 750 residents, before noon. They went to see the Kluxers and their costumes — a pile of white robes, white masks, and tall, peaked white hats. They were trimmed with black cloth, and spots of blood marred their surfaces. Saddles and kerchiefs were in the heap.

The two were told the identities of the arrested men. All were Illinoisans from the area nearby. Some had been with the Union Army; the highest-ranking was Green M. Cantrell, shot in the back, who had been promoted to major in the 110th Illinois Regiment after he survived the 1863 Battle of Stone's River, Tennessee, where twenty-four thousand died. The veterans among the arrested had been volunteers, not draftees. (Others in custody were too young to have taken part in the war.) None had been a Confederate. You can see a list of their names on Page One of the *Globe-Democrat* of September 7, 1875.

Oberly wrote:

> *(Cairo Bulletin,* **August 29.**) We entered the room where young Duckworth lay. He rested on his back, unable to move from that position. A bullet had hit him back of the right ear, another in the right side of his neck, and one in the right arm.
>
> "Did you have any ritual in your bands?" I queried after we had got acquainted.
>
> "What?"
>
> "Any ritual — any oath or obligation, to bind you together?"
>
> "Oh, yes, sir!"
>
> "How long have you been a member?" asked Dacus.
>
> "At least a month."
>
> "What is the penalty for the betrayal of the Ku-Klux?"
>
> "Death!"
>
> Dacus astonished Duckworth by giving him the correct Ku-Klux grips *[handshakes]*, which he had picked up as he rummaged around peach brandy stillhouses during the reign of Ku-Kluxism in Tennessee and Alabama.
>
> My colleague explained later:
>
> "The organizations in those States were broken up, and many members hunted new homes, which they found in Southern Illinois. This is a productive country, and its people are clever and generous; but the majority of them are very ignorant. Why, some of them have never seen a railroad or a train of cars!"

At dinner that night, Dacus told Oberly that there had been talk of building a plank road and stringing a telegraph line as a means of bringing about modern improvements to Franklin County, but he scoffed that:

> "The housewives would hang their wet linen on the wires, if they could reach them. Dense ignorance prevails among them in regard to the rapid strides of science."

The two reporters went back the next day. This time twenty-one-year-old Duckworth had a visitor, and:

> the fair girl who had given the affections of her heart to John Duckworth, overcome by the anxiety and fatigue of her constant watching by the bedside of her wounded knight, had fallen ill. . . . no "lady love" was ever more devoted than Betsy Ann Sommers. *[Dacus, Republican, August 23, 1875. The two, raised as children on neighboring farms, had sworn out their marriage license just a dozen days before.]*

Dacus lugged around photographic gear — a camera (perhaps a spanking new Meagher, like the one here), a collapsible tripod, and a case for glass negatives. The Meagher was much like a Rubik's cube or a Swiss Army knife; its parts could be swiveled together into the shape of a neat wooden box.

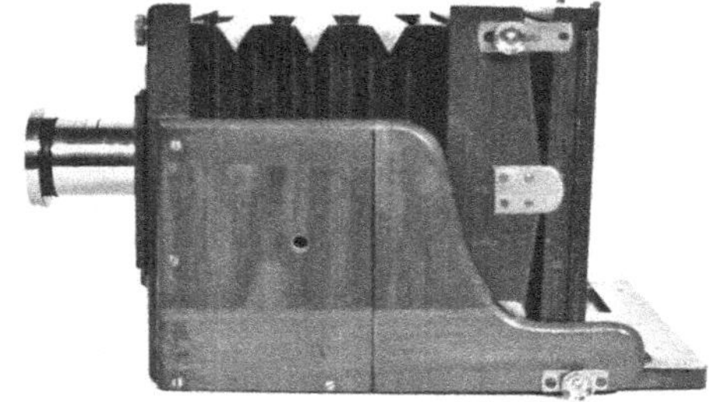

Dacus wanted to get a photo of a Klansman in his white regalia, but all the real Ku-Klux were locked up or otherwise, uh, indisposed. He found another model. The reporter "improvised a Ku-Klux, according to agreement, dressed him in bloody garb, and extracted from his person four pictures." (Oberly, *Cairo Bulletin*, August 29, 1875.) We don't know his name, but his photo was destined to be repurposed in our century as St. Louis's peculiar symbol of evil.

Dacus set up his tripod, attached to it the camera, and spread a cloth on the ground on which he posed his "improvised" Kluxer with his back to a dark wall and face to the sun; the hooded fake held a pistol and a shotgun. A dirk was in his belt, and another weapon leaned against a wall. Four times the photographer ducked his head into the darkness of a black shroud emanating from the back of the camera, focused the image from the lens on a sheet of ground glass, emerged into the sunlight, replaced the focusing glass with another (this one treated with a light-sensitive emulsion of silver), and made an exposure by uncovering and then re-covering the lens at the front.

At 1 p.m., the two journalists were in their carriage back to the Duquoin train station, from whence Oberly went south to Cairo and Dacus north to St. Louis. THE IMAGE, in embryo, lay silent in the latter's luggage.

Dacus was not a photographer. He listed himself in the 1880 St. Louis city directory as "author," living at 602 North Fourth Street. As soon as he could, he handed over his packets of glass negatives to someone who knew how to develop the plates and make paper prints.

An editor chose the best, and an artist took over. He or she meticulously traced the photograph upon the surface of a block of boxwood or other suitable tree, then used a sharp tool to cut out the troughs (the white parts of the photo) from the wood. The remaining lines for the black ink stayed "type high." A workman rolled or daubed a layer of ink over the incised surface, laid a sheet of paper on it, pressed it down with a roller, pulled the paper away from the sticky substance, and . . . THE IMAGE was born!

The block, having been cut into, was referred to as a *cut.*

Locked into a metal form called a *chase,* inked and processed by the repetitive flatbed press on the ground floor of the *Republican* building, this single cut resulted in thousands of copies of THE IMAGE as printed on Monday, August 23, 1875, with a startling first-person story about what the two reporters had experienced in Franklin County. It was spread across almost the entirety of Page 5, signed at the end by "DACUS."

ILLINOIS OUTLAWRY.

The Ku-Klux Klan of Southern Illinois.

A *Republican* editorial in that same issue boasted of the newspaper's exclusive photo.

> With this account . . . we give a rough cut representing the style of uniform which the night-riding marauders have adopted. This picture shows how one of the prisoners, now held in custody at Benton, appeared . . . . It will be seen that the people of that section of the country have instituted the most vigorous measures for ridding their State of these obnoxious characters.

When copies of the *Republican* were brought to the newsroom of the rival *Globe-Democrat* that Monday, everybody must have looked at THE IMAGE with astonishment: It was a scoop of the first magnitude! Seldom if ever had a daily newspaper printed a photograph of a Ku-Klux in all his finery, even a make-believe one!

The *Globe* rarely ran illustrations (let alone photographs!), except in advertisements, so it was hard to gainsay the *Republican's* victory. Still, one staffer tried. He added this chiding paragraph to the *Globe's* Tuesday issue:

> The *Republican* is determined to make a reputation for its correspondents. It prints a picture of Mr. Dacus at one end of a letter *[news report]* and the name of Mr. Dacus at the end. *[That would be Dacus himself posed as THE IMAGE at the top and "DACUS" as the byline at the finish. Ha-ha.]*

To keep the fun moving, on Friday the *Globe* guys had a follow-up jab, which feigned that some illiterate Ku-Klux were threatening to make a "visit" to reporter Dacus's home, which the dummies assumed to be in DuQuoin, the nearest town to Benton with a railroad. The *Globe* jokesters put this notice in the paper:

> Sir: We sea bye youre papper that you air dooing all you cnn agin our movvements nowe wee giv you warning to stop this and if you reeport this Notice to your Paper or say anything more we will visit you on Saturday Night Next at your residence in DuQuoin we will send this to DuQuoin on Monday 23 and have it dropt in the Post Offis.

Thus you can understand that newspapers of the 1870s were capable of printing not only the news, but also comments *on* the news, facetiously or ironically if they felt like it. In the next chapter, we take a look at some journalists who might have been interested in doing just that.

9 Poke at the Parade

HOW THEN DID THAT PHOTOGRAPH from a serious article about a pack of Illinois killers end up in the newspaper three years later along with the bug, the lion and the lady with a cup of hot chocolate? Here's one way to imagine it.

In the first week of October 1878, somebody on the *Republican* was getting darned annoyed at all the Veiled Prophet fol-de-rol. Every time this man opened his own or another newspaper, there seemed to be fresh nonsense about these fakes.

Was it William Hyde, the managing editor? He was a political animal and might have loved to take a poke at this new parade.

A fellow journalist once said Hyde was "a man of intensely strong prejudices. He not only dislikes those whom he knows to be opposed to him, but he dislikes those he believes to be associated with those who are at variance with him." And he *did* write "humorous sketches," a contemporary reported.

But Hyde stopped doing humor when he became managing editor. Instead, he seemed to take up drinking booze; he got to be pretty aggressive; in 1880 he knocked *Post-Dispatch* publisher Joseph Pulitzer down with a blow to the face in a street-corner fracas.

And, Hyde himself was a VP organizer! So he's out.

Could it have been Thomas Dimmock? He wrote editorials, book reviews, and critical articles. He also discovered the unmarked grave of newspaper martyr Elijah Lovejoy near Alton, Illinois, and fostered the erection of a magnificent marker in memory of the Illinois journalist murdered in 1837 by a proslavery lynch mob.

Dimmock might have *wanted* to write a column. But I've read his stuff, and he seems too egg-headed for this assignment, which shows a high degree of sharp-edge fun. And he had to handle his city editor duties, too.

Clarence N. Howell might have been the man. A graduate of the University of Michigan, he wrote "special articles" beginning in 1871, I am told by Walter Barlow Stevens in his book *St. Louis: The Fourth City, 1864-1911*.

But I will lay my money on Daniel M. Grissom, who had attended Cumberland University in Tennessee. His professors made him into a lawyer, but he made himself into a "newspaper man," as male journalists were called in those times.

He survived a noted railroad disaster of 1855, when a bridge collapsed and a train loaded with passengers (including him) plunged into the Gasconade River. After a rescue engine towed the shattered survivors back to St. Louis with the bodies of the victims, he wrote a story about it.

He covered one of the Lincoln-Douglas debates three years later.

Managing editor Hyde praised Grissom as having done more "all-round work than any other man who ever wielded the pen in St. Louis." Historian Walter B. Stevens recalled of him in 1911:

> He was at home in every field of editorial comment. What he wrote was easy to read. The style was virile and straightforward. There was no striving after effect in words.

Grissom wasn't afraid to take a stand. In the first year of the Civil War, Union Commander John C. Frémont ordered the suppression of St. Louis's *Evening News* and the arrest of both journalist Grissom and proprietor Charles G. Ramsey for having criticized Frémont's command. (They were probably locked up in the infamous Gratiot Street Prison.) Historians say Frémont was not a particularly good commander, so the *News's* knock may have been valid.

There's no record of what the *News* had printed, but that was the year of the Camp Jackson Affair, when a Union Army regiment captured a bunch of secessionists intent on causing trouble. A score of civilians were killed. It was neighbor against neighbor in those days, often to the death.

Grissom enlisted for the Union: He was a captain (Company D) of the Ninth Regiment of the Enrolled Missouri Militia, which took action against Shelby in September-October 1863, and fought at Booneville, Merrill's Crossing and Dug Ford (near Jonesborough). The regiment lost sixty killed and 158 to disease.

Lon Slayback and Grissom could have been shooting at each other, bullet for bullet, in any of these engagements. I wouldn't blame Grissom for wanting to slam his adversary, to ridicule him, now that the war was over.

Grissom could take a strong position. At a large public meeting in Courthouse Square on June 17, 1865, (after the war) he was in a committee to protest the forcible removal of three judges from their chambers by armed men on the order of Governor Thomas Clement Fletcher.

Thirteen years later, it might not have been Grissom, but it was some *body* and not a wispy abstraction labeled the *Republican* who resurrected The Image and wrote a story about it. It was a real *person* with a sardonic sense of humor, and with the right touch to make it enjoyable, or at least interesting, to look at.

Next: Additional musings, told in story form, of how The Image could have been summoned from a three-year sleep.

10 A Job to Do

IT'S THURSDAY, October 3, 1878, and an empty chase lies on a waist-high table in the composing room of the *Missouri Republican*, waiting to be packed with type.

Let's put ourselves into the shoes of the man whose job it is to write a hefty article to help fill it. I said in the last chapter that it was probably Daniel Grissom, but I don't really know, so from now on I am going to call him simply "the reporter." He is to do a piece for the Sunday paper, which will be dated October 6 but whose first or "bulldog" edition will be on out-of-town trains and in newsboys' hands on Saturday.

This is my idea as to how THE IMAGE might have become part of that newspaper.

The reporter knows there has been an awful lot of crap printed about this Veiled Prophet fuss. He has been shoving clippings from his and other newspapers about these "mysterious men" into the top drawer of his desk.

He pulls them out, stacks and smooths them. He gnaws the end of his unlit pipe. Hmm . . . everything is supposed to be so darned secretive. And readers have been eating this stuff up!

He reads a clipping pretending to be an "Official Notice" addressed to VP members.

> ***(Globe,* September 29, 1878.)** The Veiled Prophets present their compliments to the named gentlemen, and ask them to be a Committee of Reception on the occasion of their entertainment at the Chamber of Commerce on the evening of October 8, 1878.
>
> The peremptory order must be obeyed on peril of decapitation.

The reporter glances through the fifty-nine names. (So much for the fiction that they were all a big secret.) Alonzo Slayback is there, and so is editor Hyde, Mayor Henry Overstolz, Congressman Erastus Wells, James Broadhead (the new president of the American Bar Association). And ex-state treasurer Sam Hayes.

He is not impressed by this usual bunch of Missouri moguls, and he is miffed by the article's *faux* imperative tone: Do this, or we will kill you!

He looks at the next fabrication:

> ***(Post,* September 28.)** The Veiled Prophets are said to have a mine of gold somewhere in the distant East from which they draw their wealth. Their appearance here in St. Louis, it is said, will cost over one million of dollars.
>
> The commands of the Grand Oracle are imperious and inexorable. Disobey in nothing the solemn orders he has given; especially do not fail to see the mighty host and the blazing procession on the night of the 8th of October.
>
> The great event of the century is about to take place. The Prophets will soon make their appearance. A reporter of the *Post* has seen it all, and knows all. Mystery upon mystery. "Mum's the word."
>
> A week from next Thursday is to be the most gorgeous spectacular display ever beheld by human eyes this side of the Old World. A hundred thousand visitors are expected.

His annoyance grows. "Disobey in nothing the solemn orders . . ."! What nonsense! Chilling, in fact. It reminds him of something . . . .

He keeps thumbing from one article to another:

> ***(Globe,* September 29.)** The grand ball of the Veiled Prophets, which takes place on the 8th at the Chamber of Commerce, will be the most magnificent affair of the kind ever witnessed in St. Louis.
>
> The reading-room and directors' room will be reserved for the ladies for dressing. Attendants will be in waiting, so that ladies coming in full-dress can have their wrappings taken care of.

Finally, the reporter opens yesterday's *Post* and hunts up the most recent publicity bits. There's extensive coverage on Page 2; one story expressed concern about the foreseen crowds blocking street-level views of the parade.

> ***(Post,* October 2.)** The owners of windows on Fourth and Fifth streets and on Washington Avenue who have families and friends will of course allow them to occupy the windows and look down upon the glittering pageantry of the Veiled Prophets.
>
> But if there are any who are alone in the world, with a speculative turn of mind, they might confer a favor on themselves and the community by announcing that they have windows to let during the carnival. Many people would like to see the procession without imposing on their friends or anybody else.
>
> ***(Post,* October 2.)** The Prophets met in quiet conclave in that mysterious somewhere known as the Temple last evening and adopted a line of march for the grand

> pageant of the 8th, which is set forth in the appended pronunciamento.
>
> The information, inscribed on a sheet of legal cap *[lined, yellow paper, bound in tablet form]*, was whirled through the wind by some invisible messenger and laid at the elbow of a *Post* reporter.

There follows a list of streets to be invaded: 12th, Washington, 5th, Myrtle, 4th, Washington again, around "the square opposite the [Eads] bridge," 3rd, to Chestnut, ending at the Chamber of Commerce.

> As the brilliant lights and splendor of the procession will make it unsafe for private vehicles to be upon the streets traversed by the Prophets, the public are requested to co-operate with the authorities in keeping them free from obstruction.
>
> The managers of the *[streetcar]* lines are asked to suspend the movement of their cars within the limits aforesaid during the parade.

The reporter knows from past experience that big parades and festivities on St. Louis's crowded streets often caused the streetcars to just stop in their tracks, unable to go any farther. He marks that article with an X; he wants to use it in his piece.

He opens today's *Globe:*

> Temple of Veiled Prophets, St. Louis, October 3. — To prevent disappointment on the evening of the ball, it is, by authority, announced that transfer of tickets to the Chamber of Commerce event is prohibited.

> No other person than the one named upon a ticket will be permitted to use the same.
>
> The Reception Committee will have lists of names, and tickets of admission will be compared, each admitting only one lady or one gentleman.

The reporter shoves the papers back in the drawer, pushes himself from his chair, and walks to the window to look down on Chestnut Street. Everywhere, men are out decorating buildings with flags and banners, getting ready for the "glittering pageantry."

He returns to his desk, brooding, pulls open another drawer and digs down to an envelope marked "Egypt-KK." Inside the jumble: a clipping from the *Chicago Tribune* dated August 31, 1875. He's kept it all these years, along with other notes from across the river.

On that date, the U.S. government was charging Green M. Cantrell and William S. Brylie in the Brown and Maddox outrages. John Duckworth and W.W. Jacobs, the dancing blacksmith, testified for the prosecution; they had turned State's witnesses. Jacobs told the court he had been sworn into the Klan the previous July in Hiram Sommers' house. There he took an oath

> that he would not reveal any of the secret signs or passwords and would go wherever called on by the Grand Master, and whenever, to first warn, then whip, and then hang all offenders, the penalty of his treachery being cut ear to ear, and his tongue torn out by the roots.

The reporter shudders, frowns. He realizes what all those pronouncements by the mysterious "Veiled Prophet" pack have been reminding him of, and it's not pleasant! Then he stands up.

The reporter takes the stairs to the composing room, two at a time. He waves to the ranks of men at work, and one returns the salute with his wooden ruler.

He's been in this room many times, so he knows where to look: He rummages around in the closets and dusty shelves, and collects a score of thick chunks of incised wooden engravings. They've all been used before, some of them in articles but mostly in the ads, so each has a sheen of dried black ink on the printing side.

One engraving stands out. He's found it: that exclusive illustration from three years ago! He grins slightly. This is it! What *more apt* illustration could represent the Sublime Hime-uk-amuk? None, he decides, with a frisson of anticipation.

He searches around some more, examining one cut after another. He needs funnier pictures, to take the edge off his piece after he slams the grandiose pretensions of the Slayback brothers — that reb and that draft-dodging war profiteer!

The reporter sets all the wooden blocks on a tray, asks a printer to pull a proof of each, then brings the papers back to his desk, leaving the cuts behind. He sorts through the proofs, trying to work them into his article. An ad-free page awaits; he will have as much space as he needs.

Our man hasn't learned one of the new Sholes & Glidden type-writers, as some of the younger guys have done. He writes everything with a fountain pen that he refills from a small bottle of ink. In a pinch he uses a pencil, which he keeps pointy by twisting a pocket sharpener around it.

He's going to write the captions first, and then the lead, pronounced *leed.* He picks up the first proof, THE IMAGE, stares at it, grins, and on a sheet of paper he prints THE VEILED PROPHET. Under it he writes a description, which begins: "The above steel engraving represents the original Veiled Prophet himself." (Ha-ha. It's not expensive steel at all, but ordinary boxwood.)

He sorts out two more proofs: an armored man and an odd curly-haired figure wearing what looks like a veil! Or maybe just a mask. He folds the corners of the two proofs together, to show they should be set side by side, then composes a bantering comment he thinks will resonate with his audience. One by one he examines the other proofs, ponders, and for each he mimics the fawning publicity puffs he's been fuming over.

Finally, he takes a clean sheet of lined paper to do the introduction Like everybody else in those days, he writes in flowing cursive, or Spencerian, hand.

> The night on which the gorgeous pageant of the mysterious organization, the Veiled Prophets, will appear upon the streets of St. Louis is so near . . . .

On a separate sheet, he writes six headlines, one below another, called *decks,* to be stacked at the top of Column One, beginning

THE PROPHETS UNVEILED
A Coming Pageant to Astonish the World

The reporter pastes all the papers into one long strip, re-reads what he's written, from beginning to end, and makes a few corrections. He folds the package, and calls loudly, "BOY!" A copyboy hustles up, takes the offering on a quick walk across the room, and places it in an editor's basket. The reporter lights his pipe with a degree of satisfaction.

The copy chief checks the story (maybe he smiles through his cigar smoke or maybe he doesn't), makes a fix or two, then grunts, and the attentive office boy hustles everything upstairs to the composing room, where the foreman cuts the lengthy strip into manageable segments, or "takes," which he numbers in each corner.

His lads (compositors who are called "typos," informally) are standing busy or propping themselves up with their butts planted on tall stools. Each man swiftly plucks tiny pieces of metal type from compartmentalized wooden cases and sets them into hand-held metal "sticks" (three-sided boxes they are, in a way), because human hands are the only typesetting "machine" that can actually do the job, though inventors all over the world are trying to find a way to replace them. The letters become words, then sentences, and, when tucked into narrow trays (the lines of type separated and held in place by 2-point metal spacers, 3/10 of an inch thick each), they form paragraphs. And columns of paragraphs, to make a complete article.

This skilled worker repeats the process six shifts a week, ten hours each, sometimes more. And he is counted on to correct the grammar and the spelling, if needed. He is paid not by the hour or minute, but by the number of lines he sets. (If you want to read more about these 19th Century foot soldiers of the printed word, I commend to you Pages 6 and 7 of the March 17, 1875, issue of the St. Joseph, Missouri, *Gazette,* wherein it is said that "the hand of a compositor travels over a distance of about five miles" during a day or night at work.)

All this so St. Louisans would have something interesting to read and then, later, to kindle their fireplaces and cookstoves by lighting a match to the crumpled remnants.

11 The Vicinage

ALL THE REPORTER'S COPY has been set into type, letter by letter, word by word, line by line, and placed into the chase. The typos fill in the rest of the page with other articles and their headlines.

On the next page are the left five columns of the *Republican* for Sunday, October 6, 1878. A couple more are off to the right. We can't see them: The book you're holding isn't wide enough for the full seven columns.

Newspapers were not squeezed for space, as today. The exact measurements of the *Republican's* pages were 33 inches wide and 56 inches long (that's 1.42 meters!). It was called a "blanket size," and it was one of the largest pages in the U.S.

As usual with the Sunday issue, this full page is given over to feature articles, some of them newsy and some just for fun. But, startling for most of the newspaper readers around that time (when few pages had illustrations), this morning's page features sixteen drawings. Sixteen! (One cut looks like it had been sawn in two.)

This entire page is the *vicinage*, which we can define as *the residents of a particular neighborhood* or *a battlefield;* take your pick.

What about those missing two columns off the right side? We can't see them, so I will describe them:

Those two are both "filler material," articles of insignificant or no meaning, set in advance in the event the typos need to plug a big hole on a page.

THE REPUBLICAN: ST. LOUIS, SUNDAY MORNING, OCTOBER 6

THE PROPHETS UNVEILED.

A Coming Pageant to Astonish the World.

Its Details Still Shrouded in Deepest Mystery.

But a Few Striking Features Already Become Known.

Some Slight Idea of the Nature of These Marvels.

The Artist and Engraver Having Done Their Very Best.

The night on which the gorgeous pageant of that mysterious organization, the Veiled Prophets, will appear upon the streets of St. Louis is so near at hand, and the interest in that event has become so universal that any newspaper making claims to enterprise must give all available information upon the subject. The REPUBLICAN has exerted itself to acquire, if possible, something definite regarding the magnificent but shady organization which will take possession of the city Tuesday night, and has been fortunate in learning much of interest. One of this paper's most reliable reporters succeeded, a day or two ago, in winning the confidence of a prominent gentleman supposed to be deep in the councils of the Veiled Prophets, and from him obtained revelations of the most striking character. Of the general idea of the procession of the Prophets, of the design of the glittering pageant as a complete and harmonious whole, it is but fair to admit, not a great deal was learned, but of some of its parts, of special features of the vision of splendor, most accurate information was secured. Not only did the gentleman interviewed describe, as well as he could, these special features, but the reporter secured from him a series of sketches evidently prepared for the use of the Veiled Prophets in arranging their order of procession. These sketches the REPUBLICAN, with a complete abandon as regards expense, has had engraved, and with no little satisfaction here presents them to its readers, together with such explanation regarding each feature as the reporter was enabled to secure:

THE VEILED PROPHET.

The above ideal engraving represents the original Veiled Prophet himself. The artist has caught very cleverly the expression of benignant firmness on his countenance, and shown with rare fidelity the dignity of his attitude. The chariot in which the Veiled Prophet will appear is not shown in the cut, but that is because the Prophet has not yet got into his chariot. It will be readily observed from the accoutrements of the Prophet that the procession is not likely to be stopped by street-cars or anything else.

ATTENDANTS.

The above portraits represent two of the attendants of the Veiled Prophet. The one on the left has lost part of his face in an accident to the machinery during a rehearsal in the mysterious building at Twelfth and Chestnut streets. He is still well enough to be out, however.

A MONSTER.

The above is one of the monsters which will appear in the pageant, probably the same whose roarings have alarmed the citizens in the vicinity of Washington square. He is a satisfied monster and is likely to excite not a little awe and admiration in the street display.

HEBE.

One of the most beautiful figures in the entire procession will be that of Hebe, the charming cup-bearer of the gods. She is shown as carrying a noggin of nectar to Jupiter, who has just got up with a headache. Jupiter does not appear in the illustration, from the inability of the artist to properly depict the headache. Any sensible person will be satisfied with Hebe alone.

JONAH AND THE WHALE.

One of the features of the pageant will be an illustration of the biblical story of Jonah and the whale. Jonah is not visible in the above cut because he is inside the whale. The whale is represented as smacking his lips.

A ROC'S EGG.

As heretofore intimated in the REPUBLICAN that enormous bird, for a long time supposed to be fabulous, the roc, will appear in the procession. It will lay an egg. The above represents the roc's egg. The jagged fragment on one end is what the roc forgot to break off. It is a fine egg.

ANOTHER MONSTER.

Allusion was made recently in this paper to a monster having the appearance of an enormous bug plated with scales of gold, seen at night by a colored man being driven by half a regiment of Veiled Prophets into the building at Twelfth and Chestnut streets. The above is a very good portrait of the bug, excepting the gold.

GODIVA.

There will scarcely be a more fascinating feature in the parade than that of the Lady Godiva, represented in her famous ride through the streets of Coventry. She is shown in the illustration at a moment when her steed has become a trifle fractious. Peeping Tom is in the next column to the right, but is hidden by the print, a great pity, as the artist really excelled himself in his sketch of Peeping Tom.

INDUSTRY, STATESMANSHIP AND WEALTH.

The above striking allegorical group will occupy an entire float in the procession, and represents the genius of American institutions. Industry is shown in the pair of workers below raising the politician to eminence. The articles on the platform beside him are office-holders' shoes into which he hopes to step. Statesmanship is indicated in his oration to the populace below. Wealth is not visible to the eye, because it has gradually all gone into the statesman's pocket.

ASTONISHMENT AND ADMIRATION.

This illustration shows the astonishment and admiration which will appear in the eyes of the public upon viewing the splendors of the Prophets' grand parade Tuesday night. The expression is something remarkably fine.

AUGUSTUS.

The above represents a young man in the best society looking at the procession. He moves only in the very first circles, and owns more than a million dollars stock in the Jockey club.

Prof. Tice is here represented as engaged Tuesday afternoon in preparing good weather for the parade at night. The mysteries of his occupation are, of course, unexplainable. He is understood to have been engaged by the Prophets at an enormous expense.

BUTTONHOLE BOUQUET.

This is the buttonhole bouquet which will be worn by the president of the Merchants' exchange at the grand ball which will follow the street parade. The bouquet is admirably drawn. You can almost smell it.

DEPARTURE OF THE VEILED PROPHETS.

The grand ball will scarcely have ended when the Veiled Prophets will depart swiftly and silently for their home in the hilly fastnesses of ancient Palestine, to be gone a year. They will disappear in an air-ship. The above is that 'ere ship.

A MYSTERY.

The concluding illustration does not appertain strictly to the procession of the Veiled Prophets, but appears rather a playful side issue by the artist. It represents one of a number of mysterious objects seen piled up in one corner by a boy who peeped through a crack in the side of the building at Twelfth and Chestnut streets.

It is scarcely necessary to say that the spirited illustrations thus given relate to but a tithe of the wonders which will appear in the Veiled Prophets' parade. The cuts given are only good as far as they go, the chief marvels of the pageant still remaining unknown. The REPUBLICAN has only done the best it could under the circumstances.

THE POPE AND SULTAN.

Two Translations of a Popular German Song.

GOTHAM GOSSIP.

The Epoch of the Discovery of Crime.

The Drama and the Novelties of the New York Stage.

Mary Anderson and Modjeska—Stunning Costumes.

&c., &c., &c.

NEW YORK, Oct. 4, 1878.

THE ERA OF DISCOVERY.

This is popularly claimed as a season in which an epidemic of crime is raging. Never did nomenclature make a greater mistake. This is not a carnival of crime; it is an era of discovery.

A Hint About Dressing for the Ball.

A Strange Burial.

Thirty-three little quips or aphorisms, with the header "Femininities," march down Column 7 as a man's idea of humor about women. Here are three of the least awful (most are even more lame, and all are steeped in the sexism of their time):

- Fall suits are cut on the buy-us.
- A woman need not always recall her age, but she should never forget it.
- A song entitled "Hug Me to Death, Darling," is intended for a duet, and no audience.

Next left, in Column 6 (we still can't see it), are some fifty additional groaners, headed "Proverbial Philosophy":

- So close is the sympathy between night and day, that after the one falls the other breaks.
- Every country church has its stare-way.
- Some lawyers might become great if they would be content with one admittance to the bar.
- Has any one yet observed, this season, that leaves fall before fall leaves? *[Certainly a good question to ponder.]*

At last we reach the next two, visible, columns (those solid ribbons of type on the right side of our page opposite, interspersed with subheads). A concentrated mass of disconnected news from New York City, or "Gotham," plummets through Columns 4 and 5, signed by M.H.F., the regular NYC correspondent for the *Republican.*

These two columns hold the only items on the page that have any seriousness to them. One is about a grisly murder. Another, from abroad, is a reminiscence of the Napoleonic Wars.

Those nineteen fulsome paragraphs, however, also offer lighter New York piffle and whiffle. For example:

At the Brooklyn Academy of Music, actress Mary Anderson was "ringing the echoes with her magnificent voice, striding about in a whirlwind of passion." Whether she did this in the guise of Lady Macbeth, Juliet, or Evadne (a demigoddess of Greek mythology) the writer does not say, but doyenne Anderson did perform all these characters, in the same week, on the same stage.

And in Manhattan's Fifth Avenue Theater, the stunning and Polish Helena Modjeska, as Camille, "falls upon the stage like a leaf fluttering to the ground. She rises like a wreath of smoke." She is "thin to actual leanness, and yet she is a lovely woman; a marvelous elocutionist and a poet's dream of female grace and fascination."

On the far left, we finally see the reporter's banter and those illustrations he thought might get a chuckle from his readers. At the top is that Ku-Klux IMAGE from 1875.

In the middle of the page are three verses, the first of them in German. (St. Louis was replete with German immigrants who could read it.)

Der Pabst lebt herrlich in der Welt,
Es fehlt ihm nie an Ablassgeld,
Er trinkt den ailerbesten Wein,
Ich moechte der Pabst wohl sein.

It's followed by English poet William Makepeace Thackeray's adaptation:

The pope, he is a happy man,
His palace is the Vatican,
And there he sits and drains his can.
The pope, he is a happy man;
I often say when I'm at home,
I'd like to be the pope of Rome.

Then, an offering from "a St. Louis gentleman" (married, unnamed, and, until this book, unremembered):

The pope he leads a merry life
So free from anxious care and strife.
He always drinks the best of wines
I would the pope's gay life were mine.
But his is not a happy life;
He hath no sweet and loving wife;
No babe hath he to cheer his hope;
I would not choose to be the pope.

This page was not reserved for serious news. Far from it.

What about those two columns on the left, with the pictures? In the next chapter you will read them, word for word, nothing omitted.

12 Revelations Most Striking

I OFFER THESE ILLUSTRATIONS and text to you as they were presented to drowsy Sunday-morning readers in 1878.

THE PROPHETS UNVEILED

A Coming Pageant to Astonish the World.
In Details Still Shrouded in Deepest Mystery.
But a Few Features Are Already Known.
Some Slight Idea of the Nature of These Marvels.
The Artist and Engraver Having Done Their Very Best.

***(Republican*, October 6, 1878.)** The night on which the gorgeous pageant of that mysterious organization, the Veiled Prophets, will appear upon the streets of St. Louis is so near at hand and the interest in that event has become so universal that any newspaper making claims to enterprise must give all the subject.

The *Republican* has exerted itself to acquire, if possible, something definite regarding the magnificent but shady organization which will take possession of the city Tuesday night, and has been fortunate in learning much of interest. One of this paper's most reliable reporters succeeded, a day or two ago, in winning the confidence of a prominent gentleman supposed to be deep in the councils of the Veiled

Prophets, and from him obtained revelations of the most striking character.

Of the general idea of the procession of the Prophets, of the design of the glittering pageant as a complete and harmonious whole, it is but fair to admit, not a great deal was learned, but of some of its parts, of special features of the vision of splendor, most accurate information was assured.

Not only did the gentleman interviewed describe, as well as he could, these special features, but the reporter secured from him a series of sketches evidently prepared for the use of the Veiled Prophets in arranging their order of procession. These sketches the *Republican,* with a complete abandon as regards expense, has had engraved, and with no little satisfaction here presents them to its readers, together with such explanation regarding each feature as the reporter was able to secure. *[Sarcasm: Ya gotta love it.]*

THE VEILED PROPHET

The above steel engraving represents the original Veiled Prophet himself. The artist has caught very cleverly the expression of benignant firmness on his countenance, and

> shown with rare fidelity the dignity of his attitude. The chariot in which the Veiled Prophet will appear is not shown in the cut, but that is because the Prophet has not yet got into his chariot. It will be readily observed from the accoutrements of the Prophet that the procession is not likely to be stopped by street-cars or anything else.

Twelve decades later, those twenty-eight underlined words were deleted from the caption in that *Power on Parade* book I mentioned in Chapter 1. Why? I don't know. The effect, though, was to destroy the joke, to turn a ludicrous 19th Century drollery into something sinister for later readers.

ATTENDANTS

> The above portraits represent two of the attendants of the Veiled Prophet. The one on the left has lost part of his face in an accident to the machinery during a rehearsal in the mysterious building at Twelfth and Chestnut streets *[headquarters of the Veiled Prophets organization.]* He is still well enough to be out, however.

These two cuts are mislabeled, left and right, undoubtedly a printer's error when they were put in the chase. The one without a face is that sketch of someone wearing a veil or mask; that's the cut that looks sawn in half.

A MONSTER

The above is one of the monsters which will appear in the pageant, probably the same whose roarings have alarmed the citizens in the vicinity of Washington square. He is a spirited monster and is likely to excite not a little awe and admiration in the street display. [*But shucks, it looks like a lion to me.*]

HEBE

One of the most beautiful figures in the entire procession will be that of Hebe, the charming cup-bearer of the gods. She is shown carrying a noggin of nectar to Jupiter, who has just got up with a headache. Jupiter does not appear in the illustration, from the inability of the artist to properly

> depict the headache. Any sensible person will be satisfied with Hebe alone.

Even today, any sensible person would recognize the cheerful bearer of hot drinks who still graces each box of Baker's Chocolate and has done so since before the first Veiled Prophet Parade. And I'm sure the 19th Century newspaper reader knew her quite as well.

> **JONAH AND THE WHALE**
>
> One of the features of the pageant will be an illustration of the Biblical story of Jonah and the whale. Jonah is not visible in the above cut because he is inside the whale. The whale is represented as smacking his lips. *[Whales have lips?]*

> **A ROC'S EGG**
>
> As heretofore intimated in the *Republican,* that enormous bird, for a long time supposed to be fabulous, the roc, will appear in the procession. It will lay an egg. The above represents the roc's egg. The jagged fragment on

one end is what the roc forgot to break off. It is a fine egg. *[Could be a squash, too, and probably is.]*

ANOTHER MONSTER

Allusion was made recently in this paper to a monster having the appearance of an enormous bug plated with scales of gold, seen at night by a colored *[African-American]* man being driven by half a regiment of Veiled Prophets into the building at Twelfth and Chestnut streets. The above is a very good portrait of the bug, excepting the gold *[because the newspaper has run out of gold ink?]*.

GODIVA

There will scarcely be a more fascinating figure in the parade than that of the Lady Godiva, represented in her famous ride through the streets of Coventry *[though she seems to be skimpily but fairly well clothed here]*. She is shown in the illustration at a moment when her steed has become a trifle fractious. Peeping Tom is in the next column to the right, but is hidden by the print, a great pity, as the artist really excelled himself in his sketch of Peeping Tom *[who of course can't be seen 'cause his likeness is covered by the type in that column]*.

INDUSTRY, STATESMANSHIP AND WEALTH

The above striking allegorical group will occupy an entire float in the procession, and represents the genius of American institutions. Industry is shown in the pair of workers below raising the politician to eminence. The articles on the platform beside him are office-holders' shoes into which he hopes to step. Statesmanship is indicated in his oration to the populace below. Wealth is not visible to the eye, because it has gradually all gone into the statesman's pocket.

This odd illustration shows a man and woman winding a screw lift to raise the "politician" high enough to harangue whoever might be listening. The orator has hat in hand, and flanking him are two pairs of boots or shoes.

ASTONISHMENT AND ADMIRATION

The illustration shows the astonishment and admiration which will appear in the eyes of the public upon viewing the splendors of the Prophets' grand parade Tuesday night. The expression is something remarkably fine. *[Nothing more than an illustration from an ad to sell eyeglasses.]*

AUGUSTUS

> The above represents a young man in the best society looking at the procession. He moves only in the very first circles, and owns more than a million dollars stock in the Jockey club.

That jolly fellow is one of the most reprinted caricatures in all of American advertising: You can still find him in plenty of places if you do an internet image search.

PROF. TICE

> Prof. Tice is here represented as engaged Tuesday afternoon in preparing good weather for the parade at night. The mysteries of his occupation are, of course, unexplainable. He is understood to have been engaged by the Prophets at an enormous expense.

Yes, there was a St. Louisan named John H. Tice (the sketch is not him, and if you think it is, you've been hornswoggled). He published an almanac predicting the weather all over the country a year in advance. The prof's theory was that the planet Jupiter caused sunspots "when passing through the solar nodes" and that these spots brought about "great calamity" on Earth. He thought there was a planet named Vulcan close to the sun which spawned some of Earth's weather, or at least that in North America, which was all he cared about.

He loved to talk to reporters, and they liked to gibe him in their articles. His fans joked that he did not just predict weather conditions but actually caused them. The image shows "Prof. Tice" sucking down a libation through a curved metal pipette.

BUTTONHOLE BOUQUET

This is the buttonhole bouquet which will be worn by the president of the Merchants' exchange at the grand ball which will follow the street parade. The bouquet is admirably drawn. You can almost smell it. *[Not very likely unless you like the odor of newsprint.]*

DEPARTURE OF THE VEILED PROPHETS

The grand ball will scarcely have ended when the Veiled Prophets will depart swiftly and silently for their home in ancient Palestine, to be gone a year. They will disappear in an air-ship. The above is that 'are ship. *[A feeble attempt, I think, at mocking "that there ship."]*

A MYSTERY

> The concluding illustration *[which looks like a bottle of whisky to me]* does not appertain strictly to the procession of the Veiled Prophets, but appears rather a playful side issue by the artist. It represents one of a number of mysterious objects seen piled up in one corner by a boy who peeped through a crack in the side of the building at Twelfth and Chestnut streets.
>
> It is scarcely necessary to say that the spirited illustrations thus given relate to but a tithe of the wonders which will appear in the Veiled Prophets' parade. The cuts given are only good as far as they go, the chief marvels of the pageant still remaining unknown. The *Republican* has only done the best it could under the circumstances.

And that was it. Just a series of jokes, and nothing to get all upset about.

13 Fiddle-Faddle

TO READ THE ACCOUNTS confabulated in our own era, you'd think that jackbooted thugs came to town on Tuesday, October 8, 1878. Or swarmed onto the riverfront. Here are just three examples of latter-day bum information about the first Veiled Prophet Parade. Flapdoodlery!

A. The K-K-Klan!

On the internet, this 178-word blog post appeared on July 8, 2017, under the heading *Prairie Uprising* (it was still online in 2022).

> On the fourth of July in 1878 *[wrong date!]*, *[Alonzo]* Slayback organized a great torchlight parade, ostensibly to demonstrate that the community had healed from the divisions that cleft it during the Great Strike. Three-thousand men marched along Market Street.
>
> A contemporaneous engraving, published in the St. Louis newspaper, shows how those men were dressed. Each marcher carried a loaded six-gun revolver in his left hand and fully charged shot-gun in the right. The men participating in the immense parade made a formidable sight surging down Market Street – each man wore a white cloak and a mask painted to show a fierce face sewn to a pointed white hood.

> The meaning was unmistakable – the Veiled Prophet society was affiliated informally with the Ku Klux Klan and was, in fact, an organization, dedicated to intimidating Black workers and driving a wedge between them and their Caucasian-laborer counterparts.

I e-mailed the author asking where he got that fiddle-faddle; he didn't respond.

B. Alliteration with M's

In 2021, the University of Nebraska Press came out with more hogwash in a 302-page book called *The St. Louis Commune of 1897: Communism in the Heartland:*

> The founders of the VP organization proposed to hold a huge parade every year marked by military might and money, so that there was no question as to who controlled the streets and ruled the city. . . . So the Veiled Prophet was a masked and unknown person, dressed in a white costume . . ., surrounded by weapons, a picture undoubtedly meant to transmit a clear warning to the ordinary working people of the city. . . . The spectacle was intended to awe the masses with the obvious power of the rich . . . .

Gosh. Golly. Gulp. Gadzooks.

C. Do-Gooder John Priest

The first Veiled Prophet was John G. Priest (sketch on the next page), the only VP whose name has ever been officially revealed. *Power on Parade* described Priest (on Page 19) as a police commissioner who was "well known throughout the city for suppressing" that bloody railroad strike in July 1877 (for a reminder, go back to Chapter 1, Page 2).

The book's source for that was "the pages of the October 9, 1878 *St. Louis Globe-Democrat,"* but I checked: Priest was mentioned humorously four times (twice by name, once by initials, and once as "the Hon. John"), but there was nothing about any sanguineous strike anywhere. (A different guy in that issue, Gus Priest, was a court clerk and probably John's son. I have no idea who the "A.L. Priest" is who was listed on Page 7 as "Among the gentlemen present" at the post-parade dance.)

That other book, *The Broken Heart of America,* added to the stew of misinformation (on Page 159):

> Priest . . . continued to drill his deputized reserves — the reserve army of capital, as many as five hundred men — in the streets and parks of the city.

Where did *that* come from? (There is no source cited.)

During the 1877 strike the *St. Louis Dispatch* had indeed stated (in its July 27 issue) that Priest was to "instruct the [police-reserve] squad as to their duties, and all strikers who attempt to stop employees [from crossing a picket line] will be arrested."

But the police chief during the strike was Captain James McDonough. Priest was simply one of the five civilian members of the Board of Police Commissioners, and he was for the most part a wealthy 55-year-old real-estate dealer, not a cop. As a civilian, he had no individual authority over any officer, although he did occasionally throw his weight around, as when he wanted to clean up illegal gambling houses *(Post,* November 14, 1878).

Priest turned over his minuscule (and mostly ceremonial) police commission duties to the vice chair during at least part of the strike because he had to attend a meeting of the governing board of the city's new Health Department. Check the book *Reign of the Rabble: The St. Louis General Strike of 1877* by David T. Burbank if you want to be even more impressed by the absence of Mr. Priest's name in the annals of the labor dispute.

Broken Heart also erroneously said that in the 1878 Parade Priest was carried on "the Veiled Prophet's float" and next to him stood a "villainous looking executioner and a blood curdling butcher's block."

Uh, there was certainly a mock "butcher's block" on Float No. 17 (Chapter 15), but quinquagenarian and humanitarian John G. Priest as a kind of drill sergeant or storm trooper? No.

Priest made his fortune in real estate, and he was a civic do-gooder. For a time he was manager of St. Louis's House of Refuge, a charity that took care of indigent newcomers. In 1866 he had worked with the Missouri Southern Relief Association to help poor families. He was also the acting president of the board of managers of the Police Poor Fund, which provided for aid to the "houseless and homeless" in each police precinct and for lodging in the Police Poor House.

Priest was called a "champion of [newspaper] reporters" (in the *Globe* on February 20, 1877) when he argued for the admittance of journalists to a meeting of the city's Democratic Party Central Committee.

In December 1878 Priest's charity dance bought fuel for the needy. He was president of the Mullanphy Emigrant Board, which cared for homeless travelers, both white and black. Among them were the "exodusters," dirt-poor freed men, women, and children on their way from the Deep South to settle in Kansas, in emulation of the biblical Book of Exodus when the Israelite faithful were delivered from bondage in Egypt (the one in Africa).

In 1897 widower Priest married Ella Rule, some forty years younger than he. She bore a baby named Maud. (More about them in Chapter 17.) Brought into his already-crowded familial home, Ella claimed that Priest failed to keep his six grown children from harassing her and the infant, so she soon wanted outa there. He thus had the distinction, according to the *Washington Times* (May 19, 1900), of being "about the oldest man ever sued for divorce in St. Louis," just short of age eighty.

Priest died damn near penniless on July 4 that year and was buried in St. Louis's Bellefontaine Cemetery. If you are a St. Louisan, I ask that you put some flowers on his grave to atone for modern defamation. You'll have to inquire at the office for its location because his grown kids did not pop for a marker.

D. Barging In

With the passage of years, writers began tossing around the tale that the VP first arrived in town via barge from an unspecified somewhere.

The *St. Louis Star-Times* reported on October 4, 1946 (Page 21):

> The whole city and some 30,000 to 50,000 visitors turned out to view the first arrival of the Veiled Prophet — by ornate river barge — on October 8, 1878.

(At least they got the date right.)

The *Post-Dispatch* "reproduced" the barge design for the cover of its Calendar section on July 2, 1981. The sham depicted "three 20-foot arches, draped with rich purple and gold festooning, . . . similar to the ones that framed the Prophet's throne on the [non-existent] barge he manned for the first Veiled Prophet celebration, back in 1878."

Another University of Missouri Press book, *Unveiling the Prophet* (2005), informs us on Page 72 that the 1878 VP "arrived by barge, fast behind the impressive *Robert E. Lee* riverboat" and "the crowds parted respectfully; they allowed power to pass." Where did *that* come from? No source.

In reality, the first barge year for the Prophet was 1888. And he didn't float in on a water barge, but he was aboard a conveyance simply *called* a barge — a wheeled conveyance on a city street, pulled by horses or mules *(Post,* September 30, 1888). Twenty-six years later, a VP was also towed triumphantly through downtown on a barge-like float "among lily ponds and other aquatic plants" *(Post,* September 20, 1914).

And that was *it* for the Veiled Prophet and the barge *argle-bargle* (yes, another real expression from the 1870s).

So now we can turn to what actually transfixed St. Louis on the evening of October 8, 1878.

14 Jeminy’s! and Golly’s!

V. P.

Magnificent Celebration of the Festival of Ceres.

Observance of Traditional Rites in All the Old-Time Grandeur.

Giving Up the City to the Control of the Veiled Prophet Chief.

The Progress of Mankind Exhibited in Seventeen Spectacular Tableaux.

Gorgeous Illumination of the Prophet's Line of March.

Bank of headlines from the *St. Louis Globe-Democrat,* Page 1, October 9, 1878

Reporters from the *Post* and the *Globe* (those skeptical fellows) stood more than ready to chaff the first VP parade. To help them and the scores of thousands of other confused people, Alonzo Slayback had put together a printed program which was on sale when the procession began.

The newsmen approached the event as a spectacle, but some were eager to puncture pompousness as well. The stories in this and the succeeding chapter are all from the next day, October 9, 1878. I've edited them for length and comprehension.

Hidden Splendors Revealed to Mortal Gaze

(Post.) The great, the glorious, the mysterious Veiled Prophets have paid their long-promised visit, and their welcome was an enthusiastic outpouring of people of all classes. Crowds filled every available space, along the streets, in doorways and windows, even upon the housetops.

Hooded and cloaked in brown, the Prophets had formed the beginning of the procession just outside their headquarters, their Temple, a scene of bustle and preparation.

Curious men and women could peer through the open portals to see all the paste-board and gold-leaf glory. And their appreciation of all the grand things inside erupted in cheers of adulation.

"A-a-ah's!" and "Oh-oh oh's!" mingled with "Jeminy's!" and "Wee-e-e's!" and "Golly's!" in enjoyment of the magnificent sights within the temple. The interior was brilliantly illuminated, and thousands of rays of reflected light filled the space from wall to wall and from the ground floor to the rafters.

There were no solemn rites of introduction to mark the unveiling of these emblems of glory and magnificence,

> no burning of mysterious powder or stirring of seething cauldrons or wild incantations, or howling bacchanals.
>
> No, the fine portals of the Twelfth Street palace were simply pushed wide open, and all burst into public view.
>
> The throngs blocked the way of the floats being rolled one by one from the great wooden building; but as each appeared, a shout of hearty appreciation arose from the mighty multitude.
>
> The grotesque, weird, and fanciful figures — human and animal — their uncouth shapes — the noise and excitement — all offered a strange contrast to the quiet, crisp night, where the moon rolled through an unclouded sky of the deepest blue.

Not everything went smoothly. Far from it. According to the *Globe,* rowdy kids gathered at the "veiled building" and tore down the posters on a fence to get a good look. "One of the Prophets jammed a stick through and badly cut the head of a young admirer."

> ***(Globe.)*** The Grand Mogul himself charged around on a horse that looked as if it had once belonged to the Fire Department, while the subordinate Moguls pranced on better caparisoned and handsomer animals, with as much noise as they could; they frightened the sight-seers by making their fractious steeds rear up in threat.

That's where the story breaks down. Was this Grand Mogul also the Veiled Prophet? It's not certain, because in a few pages we'll discover the Prophet tottering atop Float No. 8, complaining about his thirst. And there will be a different VP as a giant dummy on Float No. 17.

Awe Mixed With a Spirit of Fun

(Post.) Small boys placed themselves in danger of being crushed into jelly by the huge wagons or trodden under foot by frantic horses. But about 8:30, a drum sounded its tattoo, a bugle called, police blew their whistles, and you heard "Git ep" from riders and drivers. The first floats moved out.

The seventeen floats were supposed to be driven by milk-white steeds, but very nearly all were of darker hue. Their lack of milkiness was remedied by shielding them with white decorative blankets.

A general crash of bass drum, cymbal, snare drum and an e-flat cornet competed with a simultaneous outbreak of harmony by the New Orleans Band. Float after float responded, and the beautiful allegory, "Progress of Civilization," was on its way down Washington Avenue.

Just back of the advance guard were two platoons of the finest looking and best mounted of the Metropolitan Police, with Chief McDonough at the head. They all held bright, gleaming sabres and presented a very warlike appearance.

The policemen broke away the great, surging crowd, punching citizens in the ribs with their clubs. At times it appeared as though the dense mass of humanity would triumph and that the procession had run against an insurmountable barrier, but the sharp points of the sabres eventually made an opening.

A line of hooded individuals bore flambeaus *[torches]*, which threw a strange, glaring light. A wild shout arose from ten thousand crazed spectators. There were the first of the Prophets, and the throng gazed on them with mingled awe

> and great good humor. They rode in silent dignity, clearing the way for the coming glories.
>
> ***(Globe.)*** On either side walked minions of the Prophet, each encased in an un-romantic dull brown domino *[a cloak with large sleeves and hood]*. Some carried gasoline lanterns with three burners each, like the footlights in a small theater. Others, faces averted, held in their outstretched hands long beacon lights which burned alternately red and blue. The air was filled with sulfurous fumes and a unanimous cough.
>
> At first these lesser characters tried to keep their mugs hidden, but the warm night and choking gases forced them to remove their cowls so that a panoply of visages were revealed for what they were:
>
> A variety of Pats *[Irish]*, Fritzes *[Germans]*, Pierres *[French]*, Antonios *[Italians]* and George Washingtons *[of English descent]* were uncovered in such numbers that a bystander exclaimed "They should have advertised this as a Congress of Nations!"

Then came the floats, decorated to resemble the theme *The Advance of Civilization,* a mishmash of Greek and Roman fairy tales, with the Bible and Shakespeare thrown in. You'll read about them in the next chapter.

15 Gods, Goddesses, and Frogs

THE PARADE STRETCHED for miles. Each tale was identified by its title carried on a pole. There were some women aboard, but also men "assumed female robes and were at once detected by their spindle shaped legs and big feet," the *Globe* commented.

I can envision the reporters scribbling notes in the margins of Alonzo's printed program to keep everything straight. The *Post* and the *Globe* were prolix in their coverage. I've edited the excerpts and cut them to a digestible size.

1. The World Begins in Ice

(Post.) The initial float represented Earth in her first, barren, frozen condition. This does not exactly correspond with the modern scientific theory, which holds that the planet came from a boiling bubble, but it was the Greek idea, and the Greeks reigned supreme last night. In the foreground stood Aeolus in majestic supremacy, holding sway over the prostrate, icebound globe. *[Aeolus founded a branch of the Greek nation.]*

Onlookers were thinking that all the ice would make a good display for a soda fountain. But the frost king and his float soon disappeared around the corner, like the votes of the people melting away in a Democratic primary. *[The Post was noted for its Republican Party leaning.]*

(Globe.) Drawn by six prancing steeds from the transfer company *[heh-heh! the draft horses of a short-haul freight service would be more apt to plod than to prance]*, two lost travelers sat on their float despairingly in the midst of the sparkling, brilliant landscape. They were freezing to death. Jerry, the one-legged downtown bootblack, asked the reporter: "Why don't they cut down that tree and make a fire? I guess 'cause they ain't got no matches, though."

It was advertised that each float would be drawn by six snow-white horses, each nag attended by a costumed groom, but those that hauled the Ice King were certainly not white, and the only distinguishing costume of the attendants was a brown cowl and a dirty face.

2. The Sun Warms It Up

(Post.) Next was the Chariot of Helios or Phoebus, the sun-god. It was drawn by four snorting steeds, the float ornamented with hundreds of gems, and the ribbons by which Helios held the horses were of gold. The god was clad in the skin of a leopard and topped with a golden crown.

(Globe.) A beautiful piece of work. Phoebus, arrayed in a flowing leopard's pelt, rode aloft in just such a chariot as used in *[circus impresario]* P.T. Barnum's hippodrome. The artist outdid himself in fashioning the pillars of the sun, which scintillated with a wild, weird, warm beauty suggestive of a smelting furnace.

3. Animals Arise

(Post.) "Primitive life" followed, again a departure from the modern scientific idea, which avers that the protoplasmic monad *[a single-celled organism]* was the first form of life.

Hideous creatures held high carnival at the base of a

ruined temple, like politicians reappearing year after year. Under their feet were the fragments of a broken table, and around were clusters of grapes and other fruits. Evidently they were in a happy state over the honor of being the first evidences of life in the big world.

(Globe.) From the prison-houses of darkness emerged various forms of animal life.

"What kind of animal are you?" a reporter shouted. A creature folded its arms and said in a sepulchral voice, "I decline to be interviewed" in tones strongly resembling those of City Assembly member Van Dillen.

4. Fiends of Darkness

(Post.) Then came the hideous Typhon *[a monstrous serpentine giant]* and his Fiends of Darkness. About this monster was his crew of dreadful demons, clothed in flowers and ornamented with writhing serpents. It was not their desire that Helios, the Sun God, should light and warm the Earth, and they were about to raise an insurrection. *[They tried to overthrow all-powerful Zeus, the dummies.]*

Thia, the divinity of light *[and mother of the moon goddess Sirene]*, stood in front, and the odds seemed against her, but she held her ground, and Madness, Typhon, Night and Eris, the goddess of strife and discord, were aghast at her magnificence. She was clothed in garments of surpassing beauty; her girdle was enriched with precious stones; she grasped a golden sceptre, and the contrast was striking between her and the foul minions.

(Globe.) Juno, the daughter of light *[chief goddess and female counterpart of Jupiter]*, cried out to the demons, "Back, every one of you!" They shook their flaming swords in defiance and, as hissing serpents, attempted to silence her.

In the background, three demons danced around a caldron of Macbeth broth. *[Shakespeare! How did he get here?]*

5. Humanity Enters the Scene

(Post.) The Earth has been reclaimed, and now humanity came forth, in the form of a beautiful maiden struggling with a serpent. Behind watched two gentlemen armed to the teeth, with weapons not of the Stone Age. At the very rear stood a centaur, half man and half Mambrino Patchen *[the name of a speedy trotting horse of the era]*.

On his back was a young lady who seemed to be unwilling to endure the situation any longer. But the manly arm of the centaur clasped her and carried her forward at the rate of something more than two minutes, thirteen and one-eighth seconds. *[Perhaps the trotter's most recent race time.]*

(Globe.) Jupiter for the first time made his appearance in St. Louis. He and old Adam *[from the Bible]* stood upright on a table of rock, apparently conversing about the chances of the mermaid getting the better of the serpent. According to the creed of the mighty order of Veiled Prophets, Jupiter is the Grand Mogul, having power over all the changes in the heavens, and he showed his appreciation by sending a pale, round-faced moon to look approvingly over our city.

6. Flowers Appear

(Post.) The barren wastes have been warmed into animal life, and now came a huge cornucopia, with its flood of flowers, foliage, and fruit. At its entrance sat the goddess Flora *[flowers and springtime]*; at her side was Apollo, with a lyre. Gods and goddesses reveled in the delights of the world's first fruits: Some appeared to be making love to each other and were guilty of affectionate embraces even as myriads gaped.

Everyone was eager to know who were the ladies that would allow such familiarity on either long or short acquaintance.

7. Hades, What a Frightening Place!

(Post.) Proserpine *[goddess of springtime]*, the daughter of Demeter *[grains and fertility]*, has been captured and made an unwilling queen. At the front stood Cerberus, the frightful three-headed monster who guards the portals of Pluto's kingdom. Next was Ixion, bound to the wheel of torture, with a huge vulture ready to devour his flesh. *[Journalists expected their readers to know who all these Greek or Roman characters might be.]*

Pluto *[ruler of the underworld]* was on his throne in proud defiance, and before him was Tantalus, the Lydian king, and other gentlemen in various styles and offices.

(Globe.) Ixion wore a crown and a sad look, and who can blame him, for his position was not pleasant. *[He became the first murderer of a relative when he pushed his father-in-law into a bed of burning coals.]* To his left was a ravenous vulture, feathers long and ragged, occasionally flapping its wings, ready to tear the liver of Tityus *[another of Zeus's kids]*, sitting at its feet.

The steps were of black, shining marble (that is, as much "marble" as the other things were what they pretended to be). Around the throne was a desert of rocks, and at the side Sisyphus, in athletic form, had one arm on his eternally rolling stone and the other was outstretched as if in protest against the job.

8. Let's Get the Old Guy a Drink

Now the top VP shows up, perhaps John G. Priest.

(Post.) The founders of the Veiled Prophet appeared on the scene and elevated their Grand Oracle to the top of the Golden Globe. There was fear that his seat was unsteady and that he might break down, but he got along without an accident. He was heard to say that he was "dry," whereupon one of the vulgar crowd went into a drug store and procured the needed stimulant, but the old gentleman was too far up to be reached, and all efforts towards his relief were unavailing. *[If this was the veritable, future-prophesying Veiled Prophet, why didn't he bring a flask with him?]*

(Globe.) The Oracle was dressed in red velvet robes and waved a sceptre, to command obedience. No doubt this baton had a double significance; onlookers applauded when the car *[wagon]* was opposite the *Globe-Democrat* office, evidently taking the gesture to be a delicate compliment to this newspaper. At each of the four corners was a venerable priest burning sacred Greek fire *[perhaps a combination of phosphorus and sulfur]* in a brazier.

9. Progress of Civilization

The *Globe* reporter finally gets it.

(Globe.) The ninth float represented the goddess Demeter, or, as she was known to the Latin races, Ceres, seated in gorgeous court above the Earth and surrounded by her principal attendants. *[She presided over the cycle of life and death.]* Here, it might be said, for the first time in the panorama did the spectator obtain an idea of the allegory offered by the pageant — the progress of civilization, for here was presented the central character of the story.

The *Post* man is not as impressed.

(Post.) Demeter, the goddess of Earth and the protectress of agriculture, was sitting in too-close proximity to a glowing sun, held above her white, wooden throne by four snowy pillars and flanked by a pair of impossible dragons with gold-leaf wings.

Father Time stood to the right, as if he had just taken leave of an investigation committee and had undergone a thorough coating of whitewash. Young Kronos *[another Greek god who committed mayhem upon his dad, Uranus; don't ask]* was white from head to foot, as though he'd finished calcimining a 6x8 kitchen, where he didn't have much room to flourish his brush. *[Calcimine was a kind of white or pale blue wash for walls and ceilings.]*

In the foreground, "Spring" seemed like any odes written to her had left her pretty sick. She managed to cling to a Shanghai rooster, the emblem of her youth *[and taken from the Chinese zodiac]*.

"Summer" was clothed with flowers from the late exhibition of the St. Louis Floral and Horticultural Society. "Autumn" rejoiced in a crown of grapes, and she held a horn of plenty, which was remarkable for having nothing in it. "Winter" was aged and feeble, on the lookout for a slippery piece of ice to fall down on.

10. Wheat and Grains

(Globe.) Triptolemus *[a kind of half-god looking after the production of wheats and grains]* stood amid a throng of agricultural deities. The float was intended to portray a section of the Earth, and the counterfeit was very good. A dragon with swift wings drew the rich, golden chariot. The elegance of blending light and color was wonderful.

Nereids *[sea nymphs]* peeped from among the trees and shook their flaxen curls in the wind; satyrs *[drunken woodland gods]* reclined listlessly, nodding their bristling heads and carbuncled noses in time to the jolting of the wagon.

(Post.) Pan, who invented the mouth harmonica, enjoyed himself by inflicting heathenish music upon the defenseless public. Several other characters hung around. *[Pan, of course, invented something like a flute, not a harmonica.]*

11. Superstition, Ignorance, and Vice

(Post.) Agriculture was next, in an amphibious scene. A pair of monstrous frogs frolicked on something that was a nondescript mixture of land and water. A team of oxen was yoked to a plough.

(Globe.) Two terrible creatures, Superstition and Ignorance, were driven into the swamp. The male was gotten up in the highest type of silliness. The female, with features out of place on human shoulders, was a Sunday-school-book character in which Vice was personated in its ghastliest and most revolting shape.

12. Fruits

(Post.) Four horses drew a giant framework laden with luscious fruits. A palm tree lent a pleasant look, and another tree held golden, flavorful oranges. Two men were working a winepress, from which a maiden caught the flowing liquid in a glistening goblet. Pretty flowers hung in clusters.

13. More Drinking

(Post.) Silenus *[god of wine-making and drunkenness]* appeared on a slate-colored ass, looking like he'd just gotten over a three weeks' spree. The crowd enjoyed it, this god as a boozy sort of chap who was weak in the legs.

(Globe.) Silenus was a satyr, a constant companion of Bacchus. They went on sprees together. Beside him danced a hideous satyr, about as ugly as could be made, and strongly under the influence of the "rosy."

14. Panthers, a Priest, and Dancing Girls

(Post.) Bacchus, the youthful god of wine, was used recently as an emblem for a Fifth Street beer saloon, but last night he appeared reclining in a cushioned chariot drawn by three stuffed panthers.

Bacchus was a young man of health and vigor, with a promising future. His talents qualify him to adorn the highest walks of life, but he is throwing himself away on bad whisky and Rhine wines. He was accompanied by several friends ready to stand up with him when he treats.

(Globe.) Behind him were dancing girls, with tambourines, and one playing on a pair of rustic pipes. With them was a jolly old priest, with a huge vessel, from which he had been drinking for some time if his rubicund nose told the truth.

15. 'Lady' Gets Impatient

(Post.) Around a table sat four young ladies, supposed to be daughters of industry, two painting on what seemed to be canvas, another holding a distaff *[bundle of fibers]*, and the last what was intended to be a dove but looked like a rooster with its comb shaved off.

(Globe.) They had paid attention to their toilets *[their hairdos and makeup]* and attire. Their dresses were startling in color, like the white and vermilion hues of their complexions. Their draperies were sufficient to cover their lower extremities, unlike some of the other mythological females in the pageant.

Their conversation was in coarse and rather manly tones, with a degree of masculine emphasis. While waiting for the procession to form in line, one Miss Industry was heard to say to the others: "Christ, why don't they move along!?"

16. Money, Money, Money

(Globe.) The penultimate float symbolized substantial wealth, "that for which all humankind are striving," in the words of the official program.

A large disc bore the legend "In God We Trust," which created the false impression that it represented a nickel, but the presence of the armored guards forbade the supposition they would be called on to guard such a small coin.

A horrible satyr was at the rear, entangled in the meshes of a web from which there was no escape. It danced about with the agility of a Dennis Kearney *[the California labor leader who was often arrested but never convicted]*.

Symbolic of the money conflict *[between gold and silver]* was the fact that when the float had been led out on Twelfth Street to take its position in the line, the near horse in the first team attempted to go one way and the off horse another, breaking the traces. It took considerable time before they could be re-hitched and the parade resume.

Finally, we are introduced to the Veiled Prophet, or his simulacrum. I would be disobliging to the spirit of this book if I tampered with the descriptions of his august majesty in the slightest degree, so I won't. What you will read about the Glorious Presence is what the reporters wrote.

17. The Veiled Prophet Arrives!

(Post.) Last in the order of floats came the Veiled Prophet himself – a huge figure, about twenty-five feet high, and looking like an overgrown cigar store sign, with a mosquito bar *[netting]* over its face. He was costumed in green and red, and was surrounded by the members of his court.

His scribe stood by with huge quill and a reservoir of ink at hand, ready to issue his mandates. Two high priests were behind his throne, and near by a villainous-looking executioner and a blood-stained butcher's block. Fierce and warlike guards, with breastplates of brass and steel and helmets of the same metal, kept watchful eyes upon the sacred precincts of the Prophet.

(Globe.) Last of all came the "King of the Carnival," the Grand Oracle, the Veiled Prophet, himself, who, from his float at the rear, may be supposed to have directed the course of the procession, and who presided over the pageant and the festivities that followed.

A huge and gigantic figure, twenty-five or thirty feet high, sat upon a stupendous throne, reclining back in easy majesty, and careless of the gaze of the hundreds of thousands that filled the streets through which he passed.

With his right hand he held upon his knee, the "magic mirror" in which the initiated can read from all nature not only what has been and what is, but that which may be.

His head was covered with a veil which extended below his shoulders. His costume was green and red. He sat in the midst of his court. At his left stood his Scribe, bearing in his hand an immense quill. Another quill stood in a huge ink-stand in the rear of the Scribe. There was no writing done, no edicts or mandates issued, but the Scribe stood there ready to register them whenever it was His Majesty's pleasure.

Behind the throne stood the two High Priests of the Veiled Prophet, looking venerable enough, narrow-minded enough, and domestic enough to fulfill the popular idea of the character.

The altar was there upon which to offer up the sacrifices, standing in one corner of the float. At the other corner stood the executioner's block, and near by the Executioner. The latter was a beery-looking personage, with a huge paunch and blotchy and scorbutic cheeks that hung down below the rest of the face. *[Affected with scurvy, poor chap: He needed more chili peppers and broccoli, for the Vitamin C. So what did an onlooker ask him?]*

"Do you want anything to eat?" a small boy inquired of the Executioner, who brandished a huge ax, large enough to sever the neck of a giant.

"I'll bet he's a bar-keeper," replied a scornful youth, who evidently had had some saloon experience. But the Executioner very properly took no notice of either, and only walked to and from the block, though his eye glittered as if he wished he could have a chance to try the edge of his ax upon them.

A Spirit of Good Humor

(Globe.) The procession reached the *[Eads]* Bridge, where a huge cross of rough pine lumber at the entrance burst into a fiery, colorful spectacle. "St. Louis, October 8, 1878," was spelled out in silver and gold flames, and underneath a waterfall of fire. A shower of hissing rockets belched forth, exploding at a height of hundreds of feet, showering downward as many-hued, blazing drops. The faces of the thousands who had gathered here looked strangely weird, probably from the mystical order of the occasion.

The cortege proceeded to the Chamber of Commerce, where a large concourse was waiting to receive the distinguished maskers and escort them to the ballroom. The first float drove up to the Chestnut Street entrance. Crimson lights glared from every corner amid the crash of music from two or three brass bands.

It was with the utmost difficulty that half a dozen police officers could handle the crowd. "Stand back!" they cried, shaking their clubs. Small boys tried to run through, but they were seized and thrown away.

As each float came to a stop, a ladder was placed against it, and the fantastic figures began to descend. The Ice King, the Sun, the Fiends of Darkness, the Serpent of Indolence, and all the rest — they climbed down awkwardly, some trying to get down "back end forwards," with unfortunate results, robes entangled in floats. Others did a hop-skip-and-a-jump into the welcoming arms of the Reception Committee. The crowd laughed and cheered, and the masqueraders took everything in a spirit of good humor.

16 And Then, The Dance

AFTER THE PARADE was the Ball: Street reporters went back to their offices to write their stories for the next day's papers, or their yarns to be sent far afield by telegraph. The society writers took over in the improvised ballroom, and don't be surprised if they were all men.

The elite and would-be elite needed tickets to get in. When folded over and rolled up, these passes were "about the size of a baseball bat," the *Globe* had reported on September 26. They "are not sold, and everybody who receives one may consider himself fortunate."

The ducats were sent to all the Important People for miles around. And distributed to newspaper editorial offices. The Mexico, Missouri, *Weekly Ledger* gave four lines of publicity in return: "If we can find the right veil, we will be on hand," it promised on October 3 at the bottom of Page 3.

The *Post* advised on October 4: "The mystery about the Veiled Prophets is growing worse and more agonizing. There are a hundred men in St. Louis who would give a hundred dollars for a ticket. All the preachers in town are said to belong to the Veiled Prophets. Go to them for tickets."

Among the small ads in the *Globe* on October 6 were two which may or may not have had anything to do with each other.

1. A young gentleman from the South, having a ticket for the ball of the Veiled Prophets, is desirous of forming the acquaintance of some lady, for the purpose of escorting her to said ball. Address immediately, Veiled Prophet, the *Globe* office.
2. Any person presenting a ticket of admission to the ball of the Veiled Prophets with my name on it will be arrested, as two tickets addressed to me have been stolen. George P. Wolff.

But if you or your dad managed to snag one of those giant pasteboards (legally), you'd have to follow these rules:

> ***(Post, October 7, 1878.)*** The grand ball in the Chamber of Commerce, a fitting crowning glory for the carnival, has been the one topic at the end of everybody's tongue since the matter was broached some time ago.
>
> We have received this dictum from the Sublime Hime-uk-amuk:
>
> - "Gentlemen unaccompanied by ladies will be required to take positions in the gallery until after the second quadrille."

- "Ten rooms have been assigned as cloak rooms, where both ladies and gentlemen can leave their wrappings preparatory to entering the Great Hall. Room 211 will be used for boot-blacking."
- "In response to numerous inquiries, the public are informed that only Veiled Prophets will be permitted to enter in masque."

These would be the men who had peppered the floats, some in drag, and all in costume.

- "Ladies and gentlemen are requested to come, as far as practical and convenient, in full evening toilet."
- "L. Pezolt, the well-known restaurateur, is permitted to open a restaurant in rooms 135 to 141 for the convenience of those who choose to patronize him."

Before the dance, the handsome and masculine Chamber of Commerce (above) had to be transformed into the proper venue. In those days the building was truly a place for commerce, to make deals, to buy and sell. So on the afternoon of the parade:

(Globe, October 9.) At 1 o'clock, the grain men and the pork men and the cotton men and the flour men adjourned, and Mr. J.M. Jordan, the flower man, took possession, with his small army of artistic assistants. Confusion was evident.

Chairs and tables were moved from their business positions, and colored workers began cleaning the floor to have it waxed for the devotees of dancing. The carpenters, who had been waiting for hours with their skeleton frames, got them in position, a pyramid here and an arch there. The biggest job was placing the large arch, a handsome affair reaching to the upper gallery and soon trimmed with bunches of sea-oats *[a beautiful corn-colored plant of feathery form from the Florida coast]*. Shading was supplied by drooping Southern gray moss.

There was a great deal of work to accomplish. The contract mentioned 8 o'clock as the hour by which the Chamber would be so disguised that even its president would not recognize it.

The transformation was wonderful. The Chamber, which in daytime is stately and beautiful in the magnificence of its severity and solidity, had become endowed with the airy grace and elegance of a lady's boudoir. Mr. Jordan said he was satisfied, took another tour, put in finishing touches, then left.

The lavish ornamentation of the chamber President's rostrum was draped with the National Flag. Suspended from on high were two banners of great size, joined at the top, then falling in graceful folds.

Behind was a greeting worked in delicate evergreens upon a snow-white background: *"The Prophets Bid Ye Welcome."*

Considerable attention was paid to beautifying the marble counters over which the telegraphers send and

> receive dispatches. Mr. Jordan used potted plants — some with broad and drooping leaves, some with spearlike tenacity and sharpness sticking out like the forbidding quills of a fretful porcupine.
>
> Above, half a hundred hanging baskets seemed to float in midair, where long, sweeping pendants of trailing vines swayed with the slightest suggestion of air current. Between each pair of these flowery fairylands hung a cage of canary birds, all good singers, who entered into the joy of the occasion and caroled forth most beautifully.

The 92-by-220-foot space in the Chamber building had its drawbacks: There was only a gallery with no place to sit and watch the dancers. There were about 1,400 camp chairs on the dance floor, but if you wanted to escape early, you had to thread your way through the quadrilles, the waltzes, the polkas. (For those reasons, the Veiled Prophet hubbub moved to the Exposition Grand Music Hall a few years later.)

Young society women and their mothers or other chaperones awaited the costumed men who began to stream back from the parade.

> ***(Globe.)*** The women paced the floor as impatient as hounds on a leash. The pleasure of jolly quadrilles, lively lancers, joyous galops *[all voguish dance steps]*, and entrancing waltzes lay within reach, and only the Prophets themselves were lacking.
>
> They did make some dancing engagements on the picturesque cards provided, but the ladies were careful to reserve spaces for those who were absent and whom thereby

the ladies were confident were actual Veiled Prophets, a presumption which all the more endeared them to the fair dancers.

So they tapped impatiently with their fans and wondered when that stupid affair — as they dubbed the street parade — would be over and the real enjoyment of the evening would begin. At last the pageant approached the building, they heard steps hurrying up the stairs, and the weird figures, each more fantastic than the other, marched in.

(Post.) As the chimes tolled the hour of ten, the thousands of guests became aware of an unearthly patter on the steps. Then all was hushed as weird, quaint, grotesque, uncouth, fantastic, fay-like, demonic apparitions burst upon the expectant gaze.

Frogs of gigantic dimensions displayed the Darwinian theory by the mode in which they paddled along bipedularly *[on two legs. And they did not croak, so they]* waddled hither and thither without tickling the tympanum *[eardrum]* of any spectator with frog music.

(Globe.) The uncostumed gave the middle of the floor to the Prophets; the band struck up Bach's Inaugural Quadrille, and the veiled dancers began swinging partners and chasséeing in the most natural and agreeable way possible. Then a promenade, followed by a Festival Quadrille, in which they trod the lively measure as gayly as so many young Lochinvars.

That introduction finished, the Prophets vanished from the scene, and the ball proper commenced. *[The men went to get properly clad, so they could match the women in elegance.]*

Newspapers gave endless coverage to ball gowns, hairdos, and jewelry.

> ***(Globe.)*** Among the most distinguished toilets, the *Globe-Democrat* reporter noticed the following:

There followed three columns of descriptions (furnished to the press by the city's leading milliners and dressmakers). The word *diamond* or *diamonds* was used forty-six times in the lengthy columns describing the luxurious ornaments these women wore, and *pearl* or *pearls* thirteen. (I may have lost count.)

Wives did not get to use their own names, only their husbands'.

- Mrs. A.S. Aloe, black velvet and pink silk brocade, and princess polonaise draped in black velvet, short sleeves and square corsage; diamond ornaments. *[A corsage had nothing to do with flowers. It was simply the bodice of a dress.]*
- Mrs. Preston Slayback, in black silk and velvet princess, trimmed with ostrich feathers. Diamond ornaments. *[Remember the youngest brother, from Chapters 3 and 4?]*
- Mrs. W.E. Bent of 3227 Chestnut Street, in a blue brocade and white satin petticoat, with a deep flounce of point lace ranged up the back, with sash across the *jupon* of blue brocade, edged with the point lace flounce, falling to the edge of the skirt; train was cut *à la Arabe.* The Modjeska corsage and demi sleeves were trimmed with white satin ribbons, pearl ornaments. *[Though the top of her gown was in the style of actress Helena Modjeska, I am sure that Mrs. Bent did not fall upon the stage like a leaf fluttering to the ground.]*

- Mrs. Dr. Henry Fisher, a superb *eau de Nile* silk, trimmed with ruby velvet. *["Mrs. Dr." was indeed the way she was titled.]*
- Mrs. Senator Saunders, of Omaha, Nebraska, in a magnificent black silk and velvet, trimmed with silk fringe and jet, and diamonds of great value.
- Mrs. Joseph Garneau, in a black silk velvet princess, trimmed with a plastron *[an ornament at the front of a gown]* of jet and black Chantilly lace, which extends along the front width of the princess; this is encased with very rich *point d'alencona* lace, with a fall of black Chantilly lace, which envelops the contour of this costume.
- Miss Susie Slayback, white Paris muslin, trimmed with lace and silk flounces, diamond ornaments. *[Alonzo Slayback's grown-up daughter was the first Veiled Prophet Queen.]*

(Globe.) The reception and ball was the grandest social event that ever took place in St. Louis. Dazzling beauty shone in the glory of rich raiment and flashing jewelry. Such an event is a great thing in the history of a city. It fosters a strong public spirit and attracts attention.

(Post.) Ladies in the richest and most gorgeous costumes, with attendant gallants in regulation black (with dainty bouquet to relieve the somberness of the modern dress suits), promenaded around the spacious chambers, while others chasséed to the dance-inspiring melodies. The brilliant uniform of the military added to the splendor.

Till the hour of three the mazy measures *[complicated, like a maze]* were trodden with delight, but at last the

> doughtiest of dancers had to yield to mortal fatigue and depart unwillingly from the festive scene. But as they left the elegantly decorated hall, they gave vent to their pleasure past and pleasure future by exclaiming, "The Veiled Prophets *sont morts; vivent* the Veiled Prophets!" *["The VPs are dead; may they live a long time!" (More or less.)]*

I don't have access to the dance card of any lady at the 1878 Veiled Prophets Ball, but the lineup was probably not much different from that of the VP ball in 1880, which included: Four lancers, two quadrilles, two polkas, two imperials, two waltzes, a Parisienne and an esmeralda.

Those quadrilles were not the graceful, elegant, 18th Century tip-toeing you might have seen in the movies. No, with all these young people in the room, these four-couple dances must have quickly degenerated into vigorous skipping matches (much like a rowdy square dance and decried by all the ballroom teachers), particularly after the creaky old folks had sat down and left the field to the youngsters.

Other dances I've noticed from that era: Grand march, landers *(folk dance with hopping and stamping),* schottische *(partner dance with sidesteps and turns),* gallop *(spirited side-by-side dance with slides and closes, or chassés),* redowa *(partner leap, slide, change)*, and on and on. By the time midnight came, these young and upward-striving St. Louisans could be wringing wet.

On the sidelines, with his sketchpad, was the famed French-American artist Edward Jump. After the dance, he was on his way home when he was mugged and struck in the stomach with a slingshot. Thieves took his wallet, a signet ring from his finger, and the sketches he had made that evening. You'll see how he recovered in our final chapter.

But to return to the ball —

> ***Globe.*** Towards morning, spooney couples who had tired of dancing might be seen enjoying the moonlight and distant flashes of lightning from the upper balcony of the Exchange Building.

So the day and evening of the first Veiled Prophet celebration came to an end, with a lineup of carriages outside the Chamber of Commerce to carry the soggy men and women home, or to other places.

A *Post* editorial summed it up the next day:

> It was in every way the most complete affair that St. Louis has ever known. It drew together a larger crowd of citizens and strangers than has ever been witnessed in our city; it furnished them with an innocent pleasure which came up to all their expectations, and in a day it has taken place among the established institutions of St. Louis, a promise of wonder and delight for all future time.

17 Conclusions

WHEN WE WERE LAST IN EGYPT (Chapter 8), wounded John Duckworth was being tended by his soon-to-be wife, Miss Betsy Ann Sommers. He thought he was going to die, so he fingered everybody who had been in the Ku-Klux with him.

So did arrested "dancer" Jacobs: This brave and quick-witted blacksmith, a friend of Isaac Vancil, had joined the Klan simply to bring the old man's murderers to justice. What's more, he was the one who tipped off militia captain Hogan and County Commissioner Maddox about the planned raid on the latter's home.

About forty other Franklin County men were arrested, a dozen of them named Sommers. On August 28, 1875, hearings under the U.S. Ku Klux Klan Act of 1871 began for Aaron Neal (remember his arrogant boast from Page 43, about "never" being caught?), Green M. Cantrell (the ex-Union major), and three other defendants. Duckworth and Jacobs testified for the prosecution. All except Neal simply forfeited their bonds and disappeared.

With all those peeved ex-colleagues on the loose, the frightened Jacobs and his family fled to Perry County, Illinois, and the young Duckworths to Henderson, Kentucky. Neal, who was a lawyer, was convicted in January 1876 of a slap-on-the-wrist charge of "disturbing the peace" with all that commotion on Maddox Lane. The charges against everybody else were not prosecuted, 'cause nobody could be found, or even looked for.

Here are John and Betsy Ann Duckworth in their later years, with their kids (photo courtesy of Larry Jones on wikitree.com). John died on March 6, 1938, and Betsy Ann on April 27, 1939.

Joseph A. Dacus went on to a distinguished writing career. Somewhere he picked up a Ph.D., or claimed he did. He wrote the 1880 book *Life and Adventures of Frank and Jesse James.* And a bunch of others.

As a reporter, Dacus covered the citywide general strike of 1877 (Chapters 1 and 13). Briefly he was under arrest on Friday, July 27, when city Police Captain Lee burst into strikers' headquarters at Fifth and Biddle streets with the savage roar, "Let every man in this room consider himself my prisoner!"

Dacus was caught up in what he called the "miserable crew" of activists, and he

> fell right into line at the head of the crowd, not knowing but what he, too, would get a blistering slap with the steel, or worse. Swiftly, between twenty and thirty formed as orderly a double file as anybody could desire, and the next moment came the order, "Forward, march!" . . . they moved as though going down to death.

The upshot: That was the end of the strike committee. The police set Dacus free, him being an "author" and whatnot. That episode was in Dacus's 1877 book, *Annals of the Great Strikes,* Page 404.

Even with all his authoring and reporting, the man had found the time in 1874 to be elected to the State Legislature.

The 1878 Veiled Prophet was depicted by local newspapers as a giant fabricated figure clad in green and red. Or maybe he was a thirsty real-estate entrepreneur, tottering high above a gaily decorated equine-drawn carriage.

Whichever, you won't see a hint of a white sheet in the only engraving ever made of this parade entry, drawn by the battered but recuperating artist Edward Jump, printed on Page 132 of *Frank Leslie's Illustrated Newspaper* of October 1878. The effigy holds a painting and a scroll. No shotguns, no pistols; no pointed hat; no truncheon; no kidding.

What's more, there was a photograph of the actual John G. Priest in his mystic garb as the first Veiled Prophet of St. Louis. This clipping is from the October 9, 1946, edition of the *St. Louis Star-Times,* and what better person to identify the unweaponed Priest than divorced wife Ella, right, with their daughter, Maud, the one holding the framed photo? They are examining a long-gone Hon. John wearing an extraordinarily garish party gown and ridiculous robe, but a nightstick, a police whistle? Nahh.

❃ ❃ ❃

You might ask, and I hope you do, "What about the nonwhites? Where were they in all this?"

The indigenous people were supplanted by the 1718 arrival of the French. Thanks to the Louisiana Purchase, the young United States federation took over in 1803. Most of the newcomers flooding west across the Mississippi were white, but by 1860, there were 1,755 black Americans in St. Louis who were free and 1,542 black Americans who were enslaved. During the Civil War, the black population soared, to reach around 23,000 in 1870 and in 1880. That was six blacks and maybe ninety-four whites for every hundred people among the 350,000 residents in 1878.

As a white man of advanced age (eighty-nine years and eight months as I press these keys), I can only surmise that it was black men and women who helped build the floats, sew the costumes, and care for the rich white folks' houses and children and horses. It was said that Daniel E. Carroll, the white man employed to oversee the parade for its first five years (and known as the "major domo" of the Prophets), was, according to the *Globe* (September 10, 1879), "not hampered by any prejudices of race, color, or previous condition of servitude" in hiring the men who walked alongside the floats. (The wording echoes that of the voting-rights Fifteenth Amendment.)

All Carroll demanded of his workers "was physique to carry the torches and agreement to obey orders." Each torchbearer was handed a silver dollar when his job was over.

St. Louis was a segregated city. Black children went to separate schools; black adults had separate social organizations, parades, dances. You can read about African-Americans and their "elites" at www.newspapers.com/image/571026558, "The Color Line," *Globe*, December 23, 1878, page 8.

Still, I am convinced that St Louisans of that era, no matter what their race or status, looked upon the Veiled Prophet Parade with a degree of pride and satisfaction. And amusement. At least one in the happy throng joined the fun herself.

> ***(Globe*, October 5, 1881.)** A 60-year-old colored woman created a sensation at Ninth and Washington avenue by getting out in the middle of the street and dancing a jig in front of the Prophet, to the music of the band.

Good for her.

The Veiled Prophet parade was an overwhelming success for more than a century, until the times changed and St. Louisans realized that the idea of a benevolent Persian monarch butting up against streetcars had run its course. So THE IMAGE was laid off from his fresh-air job and told to keep under wraps from thenceforth.

There is still a charity ball, but the Sublime Hime-uk-amuk of today (not the monicker now used) reigns over a modernized event. He is still unnamed, still veiled, still wealthy, still white. But the young women that the modern VP organization fosters (not all of them white) are more known these days for their charitable programs and educational achievements than they are for their stylish ballroom gowns or diamond ornaments.

THE IMAGE, however, lurches from his grave like a zombie when he is summoned by any writer or computer nerd who wants to use him. Within his rotting noggin, he doesn't realize he was intended simply to be a 19th Century joke. Without a brain, he is unaware that now no one is laughing.

One last question: Has anyone yet observed, this season, that leaves fall before fall leaves?

Online Exploration

YOU CAN FIND many of the sources for this book online, or get paper copies of the cited volumes from a bookstore! You have to poke around. That's what search engines are for.

To see the first use of THE IMAGE in the *Republican* on Monday, August 23, 1875, and to read both of James A. Dacus's lengthy reports on his and Cyrus Oberly's visit to Franklin County, Illinois, (the second one abridged) go to the State Historical Society of Missouri at https://shsmo.newspapers.com/image/666927026/.

To have some fun looking at old newspapers about the first Veiled Prophet parade, go to https://tinyurl.com/ym7e2bxy.

I found 309 matches for "Veiled Prophet" there. Some were in a widely copied article about Queen Victoria and one—in the Mendocino, California, *Coast-Beacon*—described a "ghost made of rags." You'll have to check it out at https://tinyurl.com/5n7bt9wj to see what I am talking about.

The *Republican's* second printing of THE IMAGE, on October 6, 1878, is not online (yet). You can make an appointment at the State Historical Society to see it on film or get a spool sent to your local library via snail mail. Or you could e-mail the museum asking nicely for an electronic copy of the page, which is what I did and what they sent to me.

The Essential Thanks

. . . to my editor (and my daughter), Lisa Gale Garrigues, who herself poked around and found the 1875 printing of THE IMAGE in *Newspapers.com*, which is good because I didn't think to look that far back.

That Old-Timey Typeface

It's IM Fell, created by Igino Marini and based on a 17th Century font collected by John Fell, Bishop of Oxford and Dean of Christ Church. You've seen it in all the excerpts to distinguish them from the main text (modern-day Times New Roman).

I think I've fallen for one IM Fell letter, the graceful, irrational seventeenth of our alphabet, which floats like a prima ballerina leading this lineup of letters across our last page, a typographical—

Queen of Love and Beauty.

About the Author

GEORGE GARRIGUES has a bachelor of arts degree in government from University of California, Riverside, and a master of arts in journalism from UCLA.

His academic teaching and administrative positions have been at the University of Southern California, Western Washington State College, University of the Pacific, Wayne State University, University of Bridgeport, and Lincoln University of Missouri.

He has written or edited for the *Los Angeles Times, The Record* of Bergen County, Wave Publications of Los Angeles and other newspapers. He spent a sabbatical year volunteering for Global Information Network in New York City. He went bankrupt trying to run a weekly newspaper in Oregon.

Garrigues has been a public information officer for the State of California, the County of Los Angeles, and the International Labor Office in Geneva, Switzerland.

At the age of thirteen he tossed the *San Francisco News* onto customers' front steps west and south of Buena Vista Park and sold copies to arriving streetcar passengers on the southwest corner of Haight Street and Masonic Avenue.

In high school he set type by hand in a composing stick. In the 1950s, he was a teen-age copyboy on the *San Francisco Examiner* (which still had spittoons near the doorways and an old telegrapher getting race results via Morse code from the tracks). A college student in that decade, he got printer's ink on the cuffs of the white dress shirts he affected at the time.

Some of it must have soaked into his blood.

About These Books

IN MY BOOKS released under the imprint *City Desk Publishing,* I reprise for you the forgotten works of newspaper writers of former years, in their own words as much as possible, but edited and curated to make more sense to readers of modern times. And always with the stricture that I must not play false with you.

I give these reports the heavy editing which had not been done when the writers dashed them off under deadline with not much chance for review.

This is not an academic work: I offer you no footnotes, spurious or otherwise. The excerpts are mostly identified and dated, so you can check the originals for yourself. And you should. Why take my word for anything? Haven't I just proved that you can't believe everything you read?

I've learned that ivory-tower writing can't always be trusted. Remember the journalistic alarm bell: "If your mother says she loves you, *check it out!*"

If you find any mistakes, or just want to grumble, send a message to me at *www.CityDeskPublishing.com.* I'll fix the mistake and read the grumble.

George Garrigues

THIS WAY TO THE FUTURE